Your Quantum Brain

Maren Muter

Your Quantum Brain

Copyright 2022

All rights reserved. This book or any portion of this book may not be reproduced or used in any manner without the express written permission of the publisher except for the use of brief quotations in a book review.

Printed in the United States of America. Edited by Bill Graham, formatted and interior design by Maren Muter. Cover Design by Maren Muter.

Maren Muter

Your Quantum Brain

ISBN - 978-1-7321128-6-5

First edition published 2023

For us to see a particle, it needs to be observed.

The human being is no more than a particle,

meaning for us to exist, we must be observed.

Table of Contents

Author's Note

Part 1—Cookies, Tea Nebulas, and You

Introduction: The Explosion
1

The Music of Life
14

The Veil
25

The Weight of Choices
35

There. Is. More.
38

The Three-Dimensional Landscape
41

Time
52

How Big Is a Human?
61

Filtering Our Existence
72

The Vantage Points of Isolation
96

Bubbles, Goldilocks, and the Three Bears
109

Brain Waves and the End of Life
120
"Raising Your Vibration"
128
Are Souls Eternal?
140
Expressing Your Uniqueness
144
Soul Agreements and Karma Carryover
147
What About Free Will?
156
If That's Free Will, What About Karma?
164
But What About Soul Contracts?
172
What About Manifestation?
182
Will I See My Loved One Again?
188
What About Remote Viewing?
190
See Other Times/Places Through Connection?
193
Conclusion: What Is Our Life?
198

Your Quantum Brain

Maren Muter

Silken are the webs of life,

capturing the center told,

where consciousness lies in wait, watching all the days unfold.

Woven interaction,

knitted to the soul,

a pattern fitted perfectly, beyond earthen control.

Seemingly blind to the paths around,

it is the fates, the Norns, who tread the life,

the measured length, and when it shall be torn.

Although there is no changing it, there is power at your hands,

for what is left, you decide,

your approach to their hour-glassed sands.

—Maren Muter

Author's Note

This book is about the ethereal and observational realms. For this reason, much of the material covered in this book has no correct or exact terminology. No language in the observable realm (our plane of existence) can truly describe or translate the ethereal.

But let's give it a go anyway.

Part 1—Cookies, Tea Nebulas, and You

Introduction: The Explosion

My hands held on to the handle while my forehead rested on the back of my wrists. Light illuminated the yellowish glass inside the hot oven. On the rack was a baking sheet with twelve somewhat evenly scooped blobs of chocolate chip cookie dough.

From the moment the thought of cookies crossed my mind, everything I needed in order to make them showed up outside my brain, floating around, ready for my mind to catch them. The bowl, the long wooden spoon, and all the ingredients seemed to come out of nowhere.

They did not seem to have been there before the thought of making cookies occurred to me, but now, everything was all there, as if the thought itself had produced the material.

Once I reached the kitchen, my counter welcomed the items. To me, the ingredients were almost alive. The butter was like those little yellow flowers at the edge of a field. The sugars were like running barefoot after a butterfly; the white sugar was like the clouds against the sky, while the brown sugar was like the moist earth beneath the grasses. The baking soda was like a parent guiding the direction of the dough's rising. Eggs went with the words from the Little Red Hen: "I shall do it myself," said the Little Red Hen, and she did. The sticks of vanilla soaking in the jar were like the trees of the dark forest, and the salt—well, that was dangerous.

Too much, and it burned your tongue and fought the caramel underscore of the cookies once they were done. As for the chocolate chips and the flour, those two ingredients meant we were almost ready. The flour became folded into the butter mixture, making the concoction soft and full; it wrapped the chocolate chips but never incorporated with them, like it could everything else. The dough almost seemed to be there to hold those amazing pieces of chocolate, protecting them in the heat and then sharing them with each bite. Warm or cooled, those chocolate chips, in return, displayed the crust and crumb of the baked dough, as though they were every bit as important. Without them, the cookie was not complete.

But the heat. The sun. That made the next part like magic.

Standing in the cool outer space of the kitchen, I opened the oven door and placed the cookie sheet, all dressed up with the scoops of dough, inside.

And then I waited.

At first, not much happened; it was as if the oven, the cookie sheet, the dough, me, everything had taken a big breath and held it for a few seconds. And then we got started. The outer layer of the dough began to melt, spreading as each layer beneath it followed suit.

It was smooth and wet looking, and the chocolate held to its shape.

Picture yourself perched atop a lofty slide, emotions swirling within your heart—a blend of anticipation and apprehension. Then a delightful shiver of bravery flits at the edges of your lungs, leaving you torn between laughter and screams. Suddenly, courage makes its unexpected appearance, gently nudging your back, and you descend the slide like chocolate chips cascading through melting dough.

A few minutes into the baking process, a remarkable event unfolds: a magical millisecond where a transformation occurs. It unfolds with such swiftness that you could easily miss it if you dared to blink. Yet, it is that fraction of time that captivates my attention, after which the swift metamorphosis soon settles into a more observable pace, at least until the encroaching heat alters the cookies' fate, transforming them from perfection to something entirely different. It is the initial switch, that enchanting transformation, that continues to captivate me. Even after half a century has passed, my hands still clasp the oven door's handle, my forehead gently rests upon the back of my wrists, and my gaze remains fixated on the radiant glow emitted by the oven's sun. I yearn to capture that fleeting moment, to immerse myself within the magic—within that precise instance when the dough transcends into a cookie.

Is a cookie the only place a transformation happens? No. It is happening all around us, all the time. Is a cookie the best representation or example of this situation? Probably not, but it is an example we can use with a grain of salt.

One reason I am talking about a cookie recipe is that nature does not do things to trick us. Nature gives us clues about how things work every moment of every day, and on every scale. Rather than cookies, we can look at the germination of plants; still, like a cookie, certain things must happen in order for the plant to germinate. Favorable environmental conditions must exist for germination to take place, including everything from the proper nutrients and soil depth to the amount of water and temperatures for germination to be initiated. Water "imbibition" (the absorption of one substance by another) allows for water uptake by the seed through a membrane. At this point, the seed absorbs water and begins swelling until it splits open.

Once the seed has opened, the primary root goes down into the earth, and the shoot stretches out like an arm reaching for the sun as it breaks through the soil. This stage is initiated by specific enzymes that are activated once the seed is exposed to water.

And then a seedling is formed.

Much of this process happens underground, where we cannot see it. The seedling is shielded from the external world and protected. If we were unable to dig up the soil or plant a seed in a glass container to watch the process unfold, we would see that one day, suddenly, in an empty spot of soil, a plant would show up out of nowhere, right on the dark soil, from what seems like nothing.

Animal development (including among humans) is remarkably similar. Both animals and plants need to have the right environment, the right chemicals/enzymes/nutrients, and a protected place for initial development. Both plants and animals have independently come together through a comparable way of managing gene expression. They all transform from a single-celled zygote (a fertilized egg cell that results from the union of a female egg, or ovum, with a male sperm) into multicellular organisms. Their ultimate form (plant or animal) and structure are vastly different, however.

On a grander scale, another development aligns with these processes, which is our universe. Nature, again, is not out to fool us. It has patterns, and we can see glimpses of this patterning all over. Patterning does not mean that it is all the same; it is not a cookie-cutter repetition of the exact same thing. Rather, we have the initial order, the created order, but after that comes an ebbing and flowing of movement that looks like disorder. This disorder continues until it ends up in a state of neutrality or harmony.

Our lives are no different. And there is a magic moment for all of us, just like in our cookie example, where the dough, filled with the proper ingredients and in the right environment, becomes a cookie. Our moment, however, is like the green flash of a December sunset along the Big Sur coastline. To see the green flash appear, the conditions must be just right, with clear unfettered skies, no haze, no clouds, no obstructions of view, and a very distinct edge of the horizon. Then, as the sun sinks under these exceptional conditions, a green burst of color will appear for a mere speck of time. When we were created, we set off a burst of energy that brightened that mere speck of time like a firework against the dark evening sky, marking the onset of creation—the creation of our very own, incredibly unique, particle. Just looking at the green flash, we can see how order moves into disorder and then into harmony.

I am going to hop back into the kitchen for a moment and get a cup of tea, pour it into a clear mug, and slowly add some table cream to it. At first, for a moment, the cream kind of stays separate from the tea until it breaks through the surface tension. I watch it intently through the glass as the cream seeps in, swirling and moving through the tea. It becomes more disordered; it looks like a cream nebula. This is the stage that might suggest the tea is growing in disorganization as complex structures form, spontaneously creating patterns. I have found, through over half a century of watching tea and milk swirl together, that although the nebulas look similar at a glance, each one is uniquely different. And there is order in a nebula; it moves into harmony. Each cup starts with the same ingredients in the same order, and each one moves into its own unique disorder until it hits a maximum state of disorder, which is an equilibrium, a point of harmony, a cup of creamy tea.

Putting the tea down, let us get back to the onset of things.

Why is the moment of inception critical? Our lives here on earth are played out in a three-dimensional landscape. Our concept of time gives us the feeling that we are on a singular path: a linear life going from point A to point B, with a bunch of stuff in between. We are told there is an optimal length of time for a lifespan; let us say that the period is seventy-five years. And the sooner someone departs before that seventy-five-year mark, the more we assume they have left prematurely. Part of this assumption comes from the belief that we are on a linear path.

When we observe life as a line, questioning the balance of life is easy; we may compare our life with that of others, and we may question the fairness of life. We may look at the turmoil we've encountered, the abuses, the lies, the choices we felt we had no choice in, and ask why? Why me? That is a fair question, because we cannot see the whole of our three-dimensional existence. If we were somehow inside the cream nebula, things might feel very disordered, and we would not understand why we were inside a cream nebula. We might start building tools, developing technologies, writing mathematical theories, pushing the boundaries of the cream, reaching into the darkness of a tea abyss, and looking for signs.

As we look for signs, we divide things into an impressive set of equations. In science, we sometimes remove the whole idea of a conscious omnipresence because religion is so closely attached to that idea. But, as we do this, we also remove the idea that there may be an observer to us while paradoxically concluding that particles are not there or that they act differently until they are observed. (More on this later.) So, with human life being no bigger than a particle, for us to see each other as we do, we are being observed. But by whom?

That is a significant question.

The Music of Life

Let us look at our consciousness.

One of the most baffling questions that people have asked for centuries is, how is consciousness created by the brain? How, through the electrical activity of billions of nerve cells, do we gain awareness of our life and the world around us? Have you ever tried to explain how you are conscious, how you know you are conscious? Have you tried to prove it to anyone, including yourself? You can try by sharing your thoughts and feelings. You can convince yourself and others you are aware, but aware of what?

When talking about consciousness, we often refer to it as the state of being aware of the environment and of oneself. We consider it through several factors, including sensory integration, awareness, and wakefulness. Consciousness is typically measured by your ability to communicate verbally about your experiences. Any variation in any one of the three factors reflects an assumption in the evaluation of your conscious state.

The hunt for where and what our consciousness is has baffled scientists and medical professionals and researchers for many years. One reason is because they typically approach their research from the brain out, rather than doing the opposite, which is understandable, because we can see the brain. We can monitor it, touch it, manipulate it, and experiment upon it. It is tangible and real.

Several "field theories" have been put forth in the search for consciousness. A field theory refers to the idea that phenomena can be comprehended and clarified by investigating the interactions and dynamics within a domain, within a field. For example, physicists use field theory to describe and analyze the behavior in a region of space that possesses a certain physical property or characteristic, such as an electric field or a gravitational field. Quantum field theory or classical field theory can provide mathematical frameworks to describe the behavior of particle interactions.

When investigating consciousness, psychological and sociological field theories are also important tools to help understand human behavior and social systems. These field theories posit that individuals and groups are influenced by various social, cultural, and environmental factors.

Bringing these fields together emphasizes the interconnectedness and interdependence of the particles and elements, where changes in one part can have ripple effects and affect others. Although limited by frameworks, field theories allow us to explore complex systems and phenomena.

One such theory is the general resonance theory (GRT). According to GRT, the electromagnetic fields generated by the brain and body are what enable consciousness. Where all physical fields in some way are associated with each other and subjective to one another—with the primary source of biological experience being electromagnetic fields—these fields have far greater influence at the biological level than gravitational impacts and even nuclear forces.

Although both gravitational impacts and nuclear forces are fundamental forces in the universe, they operate on different scales and have distinct characteristics. Gravity is commonly considered the force of attraction between objects with mass and is a relatively weak force compared to other fundamental forces. The influence of gravity becomes more noticeable at larger scales, such as between planets, stars, and galaxies. Gravity is responsible for occurrences such as the motion of celestial bodies, the formation of galaxies, and the interactions within our own solar system. At smaller scales, however, such as within atoms and subatomic particles, the gravitational force is significantly weaker compared to other forces, making gravity less relevant in those contexts. For this reason, gravitational theory presents difficulties when attempting to unify the theory with quantum mechanics. Another issue that comes up when looking at gravity comes into play when we look at "dark matter" and "dark energy." The observations of the universe indicate the presence of both, which collectively make up the majority of the mass-energy content of the cosmos. Gravitational waves and their interactions with matter also challenge the theory of gravity, along with the microscopic structure of space-time and its behavior on quantum scales.

When we look at the strength of nuclear forces, in comparison to gravity, the "strong" and "weak" nuclear forces operate within the atomic nucleus. The strong nuclear force is responsible for holding protons and neutrons together within the nucleus, overcoming the "repulsive" (the push-back between the like sides of a magnet) electromagnetic force between positively charged protons. The nuclear force is a short-range force but is very powerful, binding the nucleus together. The weak nuclear force is involved in processes such as radioactive decay, where particles undergo transformations. Nuclear forces are much stronger than gravity, but they act only at very short distances within the atomic nucleus.

Neither the gravitational nor nuclear forces come close to the power of electromagnetic fields, which have two opposing signs in their charge and are 10 to the 36th power stronger than gravity, or, in other words, 10,000,000,000,000,000,000,000,000 times stronger (about a trillion-trillion times).

Another theory about consciousness is "content-free awareness." According to this theory, people may achieve a state of pure awareness through meditation, where their consciousness disassociates from the body in a way that creates a form of neutrality that is free from time and space, a place where the body feels melded into the elements, free from form. Doing so stimulates what some might describe as an out-of-body experience, where we feel open awareness.

It is interesting to note that, in order to achieve open awareness, the body is looking for harmony rather than raising frequency (i.e., the number of times a wave repeats itself per second, as we'll discuss later). In studying these deep states of out-of-body experience, researchers have found an association between a sharp fall in the higher-frequency alpha waves with increased neutral and resonating theta waves. We'll also discuss alpha and theta waves in more detail later on.

When examining consciousness, studying the realm outside our observable world is beyond our grasp. No matter how far we dig, everything we find will always be translated into something recognizable in this realm. Even if we find a wormhole in space or on earth and we go through it to the other side, our bodies and brains are capable of a three-dimensional "frame translation." Dimensional frame translation refers to the process of translating or transforming physical quantities, equations, or mathematical descriptions between different coordinate systems or frames of reference in multi-dimensional space. In frame translation, coordinate systems are used to describe the position, motion, and interactions of objects or phenomena.

The realm where our consciousness resides is outside the third dimension. Our ethereal "overarching" consciousness has no time or space; it is infinitely larger than our earthbound bodies and flourishes like a grand symphony—a symphony without a metronome and with the mysterious ability to touch the deepest parts of our earthbound life, resonating with indescribable acceptance. This acceptance surpasses any love and compassion while blending humility into harmony.

Just like the most stunning symphonies, the essence of music moves through melody. And while elements such as pitch, dynamics, and rhythm help create different effects, the melody goes mostly unaltered. It is the main theme of a piece of music and is often the most memorable part. In our symphony, the melody is our fingerprint; it is the core of our overarching consciousness. It is our overarching consciousness's gentle, unique sound. Think of the melody as Pinocchio's Blue Fairy, that incarnation of love and kindness. It is soft, exquisite, and resolute. It does not yell and is not threatening, does not give ultimatums ("Do x or y will happen"), it is not temperamental, and it does not say mean things to you. It is the calm within the storm. It is the quiet connection; it is the still, small voice that plays your ethereal melody.

This melody may look like a transcendent form of ribbon-like energy. And, much like looking into a star-studded sky, we can find millions of stars—not just one star in the sky jumping around playing the part of all the stars, but millions, billions, trillions of stars, and each star is its own. Each star is made of everything it needs to be a star. The star is whole: regardless of whether it is a white dwarf or a supergiant, it is whole.

Now, let us turn the stars into music notes. All music notes are whole. They do not need to be anything else but themselves. They do not have to return to the universe as something else because they were not good enough before. Let us then turn each music note into our life. The melody is our own personal Milky Way. Each note is a completed life. For example, your life is whole. And like our overarching symphony, your music note, your individual life, has a melodic fingerprint of its own; your energy here in this life has its own "signature" in addition to the signature of your overarching symphony. Your overarching symphony loves your melodic fingerprint for what it is. The overarching symphony's melody is what ties all the musical notes together, creating an entire piece. Our symphony is still developing. And each life, each note of music, is an important part of that symphony.

The Veil

One of the numerous objectives of the human brain is to filter the frequencies of the symphony, capturing frequencies that are relevant to this particular life experience and filtering out everything else on the ethereal plane. This "veil" can be visualized as a vortex or whirlpool where recognizable and relevant ethereal information begins the filtering process. This process remains active in resting and cognitive states, and as the veil filters into the brain, it helps to organize local brain activity and cognitive processing. Then the brain projects its translation of the captured frequencies into what we see, hear, feel, and touch in the world around us, both inside and outside our bodies.

Just as you have an energetic signature, each incoming frequency (whether inside or outside the body) has its own signature. The signature contains descriptive information such as shape, size, color, and texture, along with more detailed information. Think of your personal DNA code, which describes your eye color, the shape of your eyes, your hands, your fingernails, your hair follicles, and where they are located on your forearm. Your DNA holds immensely detailed information while also containing generic information, such as the general code for human beings, hummingbirds, hawk moths, blue whales, or pine trees.

The brain is composed of a network of

neurons, or specialized cells that transmit electrical and chemical signals. The electrical and chemical processes of the brain are complex and involve the interaction of multiple types of neurons and chemical messengers. For example, a signature coming in through the eyes increases brain activity for sight. What is necessary for sight is not just found in the occipital lobe but is also aided by the supporting regions of the brain that are stimulated by the frequency's signature. Our brains take these signatures and translate the information into familiarity, sights, sounds, smells, and feelings.

Electrical processes in the brain occur when neurons receive input from other neurons or from sensory organs. When a neuron is stimulated, ions such as sodium, potassium, and calcium flow into and out of the cell, causing a change in electrical potential. This process generates an electrical signal called an "action potential," which travels along the neuron's axon to its terminal branches, where it triggers the release of chemical messengers called neurotransmitters.

Chemical processes in the brain involve the release and binding of neurotransmitters. When an action potential reaches a neuron's terminal branches, it triggers the release of neurotransmitters into the synaptic cleft, which is a small gap between the sending neuron and the receiving neuron. These neurotransmitters bind to receptors on the surface of the receiving neuron, causing ion channels to open or close, which in turn leads to a change in the receiving neuron's electrical potential.

The brain has many different types of neurotransmitters, each of which plays a unique role in neural communication. For example, the neurotransmitter dopamine is involved in reward and motivation sensations, while the neurotransmitter serotonin is involved in mood regulation and social behavior.

The electrical and chemical processes of the brain are intricately interconnected and work together to allow for the complex communication and processing that occur in the brain. Dysfunction in these processes can lead to a range of neurological and psychiatric disorders. (On a side note, when dysfunction occurs in the brain, it does not mean that something is wrong spiritually; the dysfunction is part of the human vessel, which is earthbound, not ethereal.)

Our brains like pattern and familiarity, which is why we often see faces on toast or on trees or in the clouds. The brain translates a signature and says, "This is familiar, and this is what we're going to see until shown otherwise." Such behavior also explains why we might jump at the unexpected sight of a twig in the garden, thinking it is a snake—our brains are also on the lookout for changes to or variations in pattern and familiarity as a way to keep us safe.

Within these slight variations, the brain can also receive frequency signatures (vibrational signatures) from the ethereal plane, including after-death communication and signs from beyond. Such signatures can come through a multitude of delivery systems: everything from dreams, birds, plants, coins, electricity (like lights or appliances turning off and on), unlocking doors, scents in the air, and much more. The delivery method carries the vibrational signature from the sender; these messages can come from those on the ethereal plane and from those still on the earthbound plane. This situation occurs because things work the same way whether we are living on earth or beyond.

Filtering the ethereal is only a part of the veiling system. Living a three-dimensional life means that we are living out all potential pathways or trajectories of this life; we are living both sides of our choices. And our brains are veiling each side of those choices and each side of our experiences. One reason the brain does this is to reduce confusion. The brain eliminates experience crossover because, as we observe each potential that this life has, some ethereal and earthbound information might be relevant to one trajectory but not another. If we were to see both sides of our choices play out superimposed on one another, they would end up looking nonsensical to our brains. The earthbound veil that the brain creates filters each side of the choices and situations into their own trajectories. In that way, we observe each trajectory without confusion, and with more of a first-person vantage point.

The brain might seem to be concentrating on only one trajectory at a time, and each trajectory it forms has this idea that we are living along a linear path, or that we only realize one side of our choices, only one reality. We might believe, then, that if we have multiple trajectories, then each trajectory is being conducted in another dimension or an alternate universe, but it is not. This state of affairs shows how intricately powerful the veiling system of the brain is. The veiling system is not working with the aim of deceiving or misguiding you. Its purpose is solely centered around facilitating observation; it allows the thought processes of our consciousness to observe each trajectory without experiencing a form of cross-contamination from one side of the experience to another.

Can we jump from one trajectory to another? Do we get to see what is happening on another trajectory?

We do not jump between trajectories because, technically, they are the same. As noted at the start of this book, our particle doesn't divide into pieces for each trajectory. Our particle is the trajectory. Imagine this: You are sitting in your chair, and your brain begins to daydream about going to the market and talking to someone you've long had a crush on.

Your brain starts exploring all the potentials of what could happen if you talk to this person. You might imagine they are married, and you might imagine that they are so happy you spoke to them that you go out for ice cream, start dating, and get married, and you might imagine all the ways your lives could turn out. You might imagine the person isn't interested in talking to you at all, or you might imagine you trip over a bunch of flowers and get too embarrassed to talk to them, and you go home.

You were able to imagine, to play out each scenario, while sitting in your chair. As you imagined each scenario, you didn't change into a new body; nor did you have to switch to an alternate version of your body in another dimension. You were able to imagine, to role-play, each possibility while remaining you. Each imaginary potential was its own, good or bad. Each imaginary potential could not see the other; only you could see them all as the observer. The imaginations were your thought processes that evaluated each potential and were able to do so all at the same time without confusing one of the possibilities with another. Another way to look at this example is to visualize our consciousness as sitting in the chair, and what we experience is the imagination our consciousness is having...

Our life is an observational vantage point of our consciousness; we *are* the "imagination" of our consciousness as it plays out each potential. We are a unique, one-of-its-kind vantage point for our consciousness's thought process on this particular life experience. Our consciousness will have and does have other life experience vantage points for observation, but none of them will ever be able to be replicated. Each particular life experience is the only one that will ever exist as that particular life experience. It cannot be replicated.

The Weight of Choices

Believing we only live a "point A to point B" life (a linear life) places a great amount of weight on our choices, adding stress and anxiety by the belief that if we make poor choices, we could really make a mess of things. And what a waste that would be. In actuality, the brain focuses on each trajectory, each side of our choices, just as intently as it does for you in this trajectory. Each trajectory is fully observed and experienced simultaneously. To the brain, each is just as real and as tangible as the one you are reading or listening to this book from.

We all make mistakes, we all crash and burn, and we do the best we can with the information, situation, and environment we have at the moment. We can stand at a crossroads with one arrow pointing to the seaside and another inland. We pick one or the other, or we pick neither and stay put, frozen in our inability to choose. Staying put is a choice. On a singular-path life design—the point A to point B life—we would only see one of those choices play out. And because of that, we begin to question the point of life. If we make a mistake, we might feel helpless: "What's the use of even trying?" We might question the point of our existence or look for meaning behind why we've made certain choices or found ourselves in certain situations.

We may begin to look for why our life is the way it is and ask, "Why?" We might question if we did something in a past life to deserve the punishments we endure or the karma we encounter. Then, to shake this futility off, we might look for a mission, something we were meant to do.

And so we search for meaning: for anything or anyone that says there is more.

There. Is. More.

Why did I put cream in the tea? I wanted to experience it, I wanted to watch it, to see the formation and the beautiful ribbons of cream. I wanted to feel and smell the chamomile steam, I wanted to watch the amalgamation come together, and I wanted to close my eyes and taste the sun and rain, and the soil. I wanted to taste the gentle breezes and the honeybee's kiss. I wanted to taste the transition of life from plant to tea. And I wanted to feel the presence of my mother, who made chamomile tea on rainy afternoons.

The cream nebula moves through the tea in unique patterns, not to make a mockery of the tea or the leaves that created the tea by confusing them. The nebula treasures the life and energy that went into the tea trees and the soil and nutrients. It moves with and within their energy. Nature is not looking to make a mockery of your life, and nature is not sending you to earth on a fool's errand, going from point A to point B.

You are living a three-dimensional experience. Because your consciousness is outside this three-dimensional landscape, it has the ability to observe your life in much more detail than your brain lets on.

You are part of something exquisite, an overarching consciousness, a consciousness symphony. Your life is one of observation and totality, meaning you are experiencing everything your life has to offer. And because you are experiencing everything, harmony is created, and that harmony becomes stunningly, beautifully, and significantly whole, total, and complete.

The Three-Dimensional Landscape

As discussed above, the human life experience is three-dimensional. Some people may add time as a fourth dimension. But as we experience time here on earth, we find it is still part of the third. Time is a descriptive concept; it is a measurement. When we leave our earthbound life, time no longer exists, at least not the way it does for us now.

Have you ever tried to pin a moment of time down?

For fun, just say, "Right now," and that "Right now" has long passed by the time it leaves your lips. It has long passed by the time your brain has conjured it up. We cannot stop the wave of energy that is us. We would need to stop this wave, and all the energy connected to it, to live in the "now."

In fact, every moment has already passed by before you even register it. Like thunder trailing lightning, the clash lags the bolt. Even when the bolt is right in front of you, there is still a lag. As we think about this, we will find there is no "now" and that every single moment is an isolated existence. These moments are woven together with all the different moments, becoming a wave that helps us move through the measurement of time. This wave of experiential-trajectory moments helps shape our perspective of life. Part of the perspective of life includes our perspective of others and the trust and love we have for ourselves.

Each moment we can observe contains smaller moments, and those smaller moments contain smaller moments, and so forth. We cannot stop or pause at any moment. There are some thoughts, like those of the theoretical physicist Julian Barbour, that say the passing of time is an illusion. That each moment we ever live, from birth to death, and everything in between, is like a photograph or painting, and every moment is isolated and exists independently forever.

When we look at time a little later in this book, we'll see it is a third-dimensional tool that does exist as we perceive it here on this plane. For this reason, all those isolated moments of our life do not remain eternally in "photographs" for review, but they remain as part of a whole. The moment helps create the depth and resonance of this life experience upon its completion (the ceasing of the physical body).

As we conceptualize drilling down into these single points, trying to pause them, we'll find that we cannot. So let's look at dimensions. We'll start with a zero-dimensional solitary tiny dot, the tiniest pinpoint. The point has no physical size; if you were to zoom in and out, it would look the same, with no change in size, regardless if it were closer to you or farther away. It would not get bigger or smaller; it would just look the same, and it would still be a dot. Hypothetically, the only way to observe this dot is through the first dimension; observation from zero dimensions is not possible.

The first dimension is a series of zero-dimensional points lined together, creating a straight line. If observation were possible, there would be only one way to observe life along the line of the first dimension; you'd need to be in it. Being in the first dimension means being inside the line. Your observation would be in one direction, with no way to go up or down or any variation from that, no left-to-right / right-to-left movement. And, with no left or right, or up or down, there is also no turning around to go in any direction. Observation is unidirectional.

The only objects in the first dimension that exist are a point and a line. If a particle lived in the first dimension and had a way to see (if it had eyes, for example), then the only thing it could see would be the point or the dot of the zero dimension. Again, the dot would not get bigger or smaller. It would be a dot. The particle's ability to see this dot of the zero dimension occurs because it lives inside the line of the first. It cannot go out of the line. It cannot step back to see the line. It can only be in the line, and the only thing it can see is the solitary point of the zero dimension.

There is also no way to travel along the line because there is no measurement of time. If observation were possible, then observation would always only see a point or dot.

To try and imagine this scenario further, take a dowel and pretend you are inside it. To do this, lift it up and look at the cut end of the dowel and step inside. Now imagine that the cut end of the dowel is a dot, and it will always be the exact distance from your eyes. Pretend you cannot see around the dowel or look down its shaft; the only thing you can see is the flat cut edge of the end of the dowel against the pure black of nothingness. You cannot even see the pure black of nothingness—there is no context of the dowel's surroundings or environment. And there is no location for observation to go. There is no location for observation to be. The only thing for observation to see would be the same dot of the cut end of the dowel; an observer cannot look up or down or side to side. The observation particle living in the first dimension can only see the zero dimension because it resides inside the first dimension.

Now, let us bring the particle to live in the second dimension. To create the second dimension, we will bring a bunch of the lines of the first dimension together, creating a flat world, just flat. Think of the top of a piece of paper—not the bottom, just the top of a piece of paper. These flat paper tops can be any shape: rectangular, triangular, circular, octagonal, hexagonal... They can be any flat shape, and there are no sides or bottoms or in between. Now, if our particle lived inside the shaped second dimension, what would it see? Only a line.

Let us take our paper and pretend we are inside it. Lift it up and look at its edge, the edge of the paper only against the pure black of nothingness—no context of its surroundings or environment. Not the top or bottom of the paper, because they do not exist in the second dimension. For this reason, and a few other factors, no matter what shape it is, our second-dimension particle can only see a line segment of the first dimension. This is because our particle lives inside the second. It has no depth perception, no shadowing, just a line.

If the particle looked at a circle, then its perception of the line segment would be the width of the diameter of the circle. The particle would not see any edge closer to it; it would not see the arch of the circle—just a straight line. And because it would never be able to see anything but the line segment, it would never be able to know what the shapes look like because it cannot step back to draw the shapes—its second-dimension "brain" does not have the ability to draw out the lines; it does not have the ability to garner any more information than a line. The particle can only see the line of the first dimension, since it lives inside the second dimension.

A particle living in the third dimension gets to see the shapes of the second; it can see the shape of a triangle and the form of a tree. It can also see to the left and right and up and down. It gets to see the design on the outside of the shapes, too. For example, if it were a pine tree, it could see the color and texture, but it could not see into the tree or through the tree, nor could it see the whole tree. If it were a cube, the particle could only see the side of the cube facing it, no matter how it was angled. If it were angled at a slant and slightly turned, the particle would only see the part of each side incorporated into the angle that faces it, creating a two-dimensional shape.

But why does it seem that we see in three dimensions? Seeing in 3D is just the visual cortex (the primary cortical region of the brain that receives, integrates, and processes visual information relayed from the retinas) blending the second dimension with depth information, including the value of time. The measurement of time allows us to move within the three-dimensional landscape. Time also gives us the ability to sense the empty space between objects, which helps us understand their shapes and proximity to us and to each other. In conjunction with our ability to add depth through shadowing, time allows the things we see, the tangible objects, to seem as though they are popping out at us, as in a 3D movie. We call it seeing in three dimensions because that is where we live.

Your brain constantly adjusts to your surroundings and circumstances by taking your actions and the environment's actions into account. It considers the frequencies of energetic wave movement. The more rapid the frequency, the denser the energy is, and your brain translates that into a solid. At conception, we become both a wave and a finite particle. The concept of "finite" is crucial because it helps give perimeters to observation and gives our human life the role of experience. Our human experience is prepped before conception with every experience leading up to it, and with every experience after it. It is the moment of our inception where our particular life begins; observational material comes into existence. At this inception, our expiration date and every moment, every possibility in between, are realized; they happen simultaneously. Just as where there is a front, there is a back, where there is an up, there is a down, and where we have a conception, there is death; one does not exist without the other. And they bloom together, along with all the in-betweens.

Time

This letter, which I wrote when I was eight years old, is one of hundreds of letters I buried in the 1970s in a forest meadow at my childhood home outside Portland, Oregon. When I later unearthed the letters, I found that I'd addressed almost all of them to the "Flower Lady."

Dear Flower Lady,

Today we are looking at time. I say looking

because if we don't look at it, it's not there. It is kind of weird that way. Like I was already dead when I was born. In order for me to be born, I needed to die at the exact same time. And all the things I do, going to gymnastics, playing the violin, eating berries in the field, and dad coming to school, all happened at the same time. What I want to know about time isn't whether it is there or not because even because we can have it, it's not what we think it is. I can go to sleep one night and the night lasts forever. I can go to sleep on another night, and I just blink my eyes, and it's over. Really truly. Remember that one time I told you about it? I put my head on the pillow, blinked one time, and it was morning. Or how about when we are playing, and time just kind of stops, and you look around, and wonder, did everything disappear? But why does our brain slow time down so much that we can do all of this stuff? There is a lot more

to this, don't you think? Time is not what it seems.

From the chocolate covered daydream,

Me

Part of three-dimensional life comes with the measurement of time. While people say it cannot be altered, have you ever had time slow to a stop, like when your heart catches or your lungs clench? We may not be able to stop our hearts and lungs from working without dying, but we can slow them down or speed them up. And believe it or not, the same is true with time.

Just like with our shared or common reality, we have a common idea of time. We also have individual time, where certain events are slowed for us, while the common time continues at its common rate. When our individual time alters, we may get the sensation of having stood outside the common reality, watching it progress while our time stands still. Sometimes this happens when you have a great emotional heart-stopping experience, where if you continued, at that moment, along with the common time, it would place extraordinary energetic pressure upon your body, primarily your heart. Picture pressure like deep diving without a mini-submarine, where if you continued with the common rate of time, you'd experience so much energy that it could short-circuit you. So, your individual time temporarily slows, allowing your brain to process and giving your body the chance to brace itself. This does not always have to be a heart-stopping event. Our individual time can vary when we have new or fresh exposure or new or fresh sensations such as childhood days, where they linger.

Time can also speed up individually. Your day may have flown by, while someone else's may have lingered. Outside our observation, time is not a singular direction. Time is part of the very fabric of our observable universe. We're told that in space, the faster we go, the slower our time is. The speed of light is part of our observational time, but much "faster" speeds exist, so much faster that time no longer exists. After all, time does not exist outside this third-dimensional plane. It exists as we observe it—and our observational perspective is from the third dimension.

The time we use and associate with our life experience here on earth allows us to move around our three-dimensional life. It enables us to walk around trees or around each other. Time is a measurement of length. It helps create human reality, allowing our brains to process interactions and observations.

Without our observation, particles "play" differently. They can move both left and right, up and down, and everywhere simultaneously because the particles do not adhere to any label. They only become up and down, left and right, here and there, when we measure them. When we watch them, when we observe them, the space they're "traveling" in collapses, and they present themselves to fit the observation, like a game of musical chairs or, better yet, "red light, green light."

Our life experience includes (among other things) a combination of forms of the theories of quantum superposition, quantum entanglement, and the principle of least action. (I'll explain these terms later.) I say forms of these theories (and others) because by naming them, by mathematically researching them, we are observing them. And when we observe them, we are isolating their true meanings. Words and descriptions are as limiting as those observations are. For example, imagine I invite you into a dark room. We will pretend it's lunchtime, and you happen to have an apple with you, which I did not know. While you're in the dark room, you start to eat the apple. And right at that moment, I flash a light on you, quickly on and quickly off, and I see you with the apple to your lips. Then, from that point forward, I'll tell everyone that your hand was glued to your face with an apple. I can draw it out and prove it mathematically. I may make additional theories about the gluing capability of apples, write equations, and then test them. I may see you with another glued apple or I may not; both would help my exploration of the phenomenon of apple gluing. My question to you now is this: Do you ever do anything else besides either gluing your hand and face together with an apple or not gluing your hand and face together with an apple? Is there much more to you than that?

"Quantum superposition" happens faster than the speed of light and is a fundamental concept in quantum mechanics that describes the ability of quantum particles to exist in multiple states or configurations simultaneously. Quantum particles can exist in a combination or superposition of different states at the same time.

The superposition allows the particle to exhibit wave-like properties, such as interference and the ability to occupy multiple positions or energy levels simultaneously. Quantum interference is a phenomenon that occurs when two or more quantum waves interact with each other, resulting in either reinforcement or cancellation of their amplitudes. In simple terms, this is similar to the interference pattern observed when two waves, such as water waves or sound waves, meet and either amplify or cancel each other out.

When we measure or observe a particle in superposition, it collapses into one of its possible states, referred to as the measurement outcome. The probability of obtaining a particular outcome is determined by the amplitudes associated with the different states in the superposition.

Quantum superposition is a key feature of quantum systems and plays a vital role in phenomena such as quantum entanglement and quantum computing. Such superposition has been experimentally verified through various experiments, confirming the probabilistic nature of quantum mechanics and the coexistence of multiple states until measurement occurs.

When we observe the speed of light through our common perspective, the observation of the light collapses something much greater into a wave of light. Even the famed theoretical physicist Albert Einstein was baffled by this phenomenon, dismissing it as "spooky action at a distance."

How Big Is a Human?

Particles have positions. In our observation of particles, they move in a straight line until something else (another particle) collides with them and changes their direction. You may think I am silly in suggesting that our bodies are but mere particles, because a human being seems much larger than a particle. But we need to look at this idea from a universal vantage point. Let us pretend that the universe is the largest museum in the world.

From the front door, we'll pretend that the whole museum is the observable universe, estimated at 93 billion light-years in diameter. Light travels at a speed of approximately 299,792 kilometers per second (or about 186,282 miles per second, or 7.48 times around the earth). In one year, light can cover a distance of about 9.46 trillion kilometers (or about 5.88 trillion miles). If we step inside a little more, we'll see the museum wings leading us toward different galleries, which is like cosmic "webbing." Let us move toward one of the wings. This one is like a supercluster complex of galaxies almost a billion light-years long, and it looks like an incredible filament of supercluster galaxies. In one of the filament branches, or branches of the wing, is the Virgo Supercluster, at a distance of millions of light-years inside this supercluster. You'll see a smaller cluster of fifty to sixty galaxies; this is an exhibition room in the museum. In this cluster of galaxies, you will find the Milky Way galaxy (not the chocolate bar, but that sounds good). The Milky Way, being 100,000 light-years across, is the second-largest galaxy in this cluster we share the exhibition with.

You may have admired the Milky Way glowing against a dark evening sky, so you'll know it is a gorgeous star-studded galaxy ribboning above us (from our vantage point) as it swirls in the universe. (Now I am really thinking of a churning vat of melted chocolate, and I may need to take a break and sample some.)

Tucked away in the Milky Way is a local interstellar cloud, a small landscape painting on the gallery wall. As we step up to this painting, we must engage our imagination a bit more to find a seeded dandelion on a hillside, so small again that it is barely there. On top of one of the soft white tufts, on this microscopic dandelion, you will find a seed. That speck of imaginary seed will be the earth. Zooming in on the earth, you'll start to see the continents and surrounding waters. Magnifying your imaginary earth even further, you'll find your continent, your country, your town; and even closer, your street; even closer, your house; even closer, you.

Now, go all the way back to the beginning, through the wings and collections, and all the way back to the entrance. From that viewpoint, a human is smaller than a quantum measurement; it is a particle inside a particle, which is inside a particle … and so forth, an untold million times over. From this vantage point, human beings do not exist. We are no more visible than a quark or boson is to the naked human eye: in fact, even less so. And even the quark and the boson have smaller particles that are a part of them, and those particles have even smaller ones yet, just as the human body is comprised of subparticles.

The particles that are us—me for me, and you for you—are a compilation of particles dancing around each other, creating movement. Just as our conception has death, our particles have waves, and our waves have particles. One is the other, just as the other is one.

The vibration of our inner particles helps dictate the density of the various parts of our bodies. Our bones have less intermolecular space, exude less energy, and have a more fixed or rigid shape than the other body parts. You may touch your hands, and your brain says, "solid," but they are not. Not even your bones or the granite cliffs of majestic mountains are truly solid. They are abuzz with vibrating elements flowing through, passing by, and weaving us all together.

When particles show up in our labs or in mathematics, or because they were brought to our attention, it is because we are considering them, observing them. And that observation allows them to exist in form.

The brain's ability to translate information that is outside its normal translation of relevancy can be quite bizarre. We can hear of these bizarre results in frightening near-death experiences (NDEs). The translation of the ethereal realm outside this body can overwhelm the brain. Outside this body, time does not exist; eternity is the absence of time; it is the absence of measurement as we know it. The universe does not exist as it does in this human, earthbound perspective. In this absence of time and space is where our consciousnesses reside—all of them, yours, mine, and those from every walk of life—and not only from earth.

The information and interaction that is part of this veiled ethereal plane can overwhelm the brain upon reanimation, where it comes back to this life. You may have felt as though you were on the other side of the brain's veil for hours, for months, for an entire lifetime during your NDE. You may have hovered over your body; you may have looked around and seen and heard those trying to help you. That hovering was your transition out of the brain's veil; you were still viable and focused on this life experience. It's when the hovering sensation stopped and moved into the darkness or light that you breached the barrier. Sometimes this transition is instantaneous, and you do not have that hovering sensation. And whether you had that hovering experience or not, once you left your brain's veil, the experience was not timed or measured. It just was.

The other side is filled with a depth that is indescribable; it is a harmonic state where there is no fear, no pain, and it is comprised of something far beyond love. Far beyond compassion. Far beyond anything imaginable in our current life. When we enter that state from this life through an out-of-body or near-death experience, many times the fundamental way in which we view life upon our return changes. These changes include a loss of fear of death and an understanding that there is life after death, increased compassion, and love for others. People often experience an altered perspective on materialism, a removed inhibition to share their feelings. A deeper appreciation for life. At the same time, they may struggle to reacclimate to this life and want to go back, "to go home."

I recently had a woman write to me who tried her best to describe the feeling of her experience, and I thought it was beautiful. One of the reasons it touched my heart was that her description also encapsulated the innocence and vulnerability that are integral parts of this ethereal love. This is what she said: "You are loved with a feeling of all-encompassing comfort and joy and warmth. I can only describe it as when you get sheets and towels right out of the dryer. That warmth that penetrates to the bones."

The time when your consciousness returns to focusing on your body after a near-death experience is when the brain reanimates to this life and begins the veiling process once again. This veiling process is instant, and it begins to translate, to the best of its ability, where you were. This process makes it feel as if the experience translation your brain is showing you is where you were the whole time. Your brain shows white clouds and angels, or buildings, or libraries of records, of messages or conversations, of scrumptious foods, abundance, and peace throughout the lands, but that is all your brain's best ability regarding the ethereal translation.

Sometimes the translation becomes very dark, where the experience looks more like hell than anything else. Where your heart races and nightmares creep, and the cold hand of death reaches for you upon your return. Where wretched screams fill the air—or, maybe, it is just pure darkness, an eternity with your thoughts and nothing else. That is all your brain's translation. We must remember that the brain has an incredible imagination. It takes nonrelevant ethereal frequencies and translates them into what it thinks they should be. Sometimes what we experience on the other side of the veil is something we were told at some point in our life does not exist, or it is wrong. Or the experience does not match what we thought it should. Maybe we thought it would be tangible, that there would be streets, buildings, the earth, but bountiful and clean, with no war, a paradise. This does not mean your experience was as dark as your brain's description; what you are remembering is your brain translating things into relevancy. Maybe it thought, "Yes, a field of piranha-headed flowers is perfect." This is similar to when we enter a new situation, and at first the situation is scary but then it turns out to be fairly good after all. We were scared because it was something unknown, something unfamiliar. And the piranha-headed flowers turn out to be soothing foot- and back scratchers.

The brain's attempt to translate the ethereal

is a massive undertaking. Our bodies are mere particles on the grand scale of things, so when we turn our focus away from the earthbound stage, we can find the experience quite overwhelming. The magnitude of information and belonging and connection is beyond translation, leaving your brain speechless while your heart remembers through melody.

Filtering Our Existence

For a moment, pretend you are driving in the car, and every single radio station in the world is coming out on one channel all at the same time. And you do not get to turn it off, and you cannot make one station louder than the other. You cannot change the languages to English. You cannot alter them; they all come out in equal measure, creating intense nonsensical noise.

If we pretend that ethereal frequencies are the radio

stations, we can see why the human brain creates the veil. Because even though we are connected to these ethereal frequencies, the majority of them are not relevant to this particular life experience. The life experience we have right now doesn't need all of that information in the forefront of the brain, so the brain creates the veil to help distinguish the relevant information from the nonrelevant. Otherwise, like our ethereal radio station playing every single frequency at the same time, our experience here would be chaotic, like the screeching of mermaid eggs on land.

When we look at the entanglement of the earthbound and the ethereal realms (I am considering the universe part of the earthbound plane because we can observe it), there is no distance, no separation between these realms. We are inside, we are a woven part of the ethereal. There is no division, only a veiling system helping us make sense of the innumerable vibrational waves communicating with our bodies.

Just as the frequencies interact with your body, your body interacts with them from both inside and outside your body. This veiled communication determines how you experience the world around you by evaluating vibrational signatures. This evaluation process is also what creates the "veil."

The brain is like the last layer of the human life experience filtration system. The stimulus comes in and activates the initial analysis, which, for the most part, occurs outside the skull. The brain's job is mechanical in the grand scheme of things. Its primary function is to protect the human body for as long as it can. It constantly adjusts to what it feels is relevant to our life experiences. And sometimes, information slips through the brain's filter because it looks, temporarily, relevant at first glance.

The veil is the brain's fishing net.

Our veil system says, "Is this somewhat

recognizable to human life?" If it is, then the information continues to the next layer of filtration, eventually coming to a layer where your brain deems the information relevant to your current life experience. Then it acts accordingly. If it allows information through the veil that turns out not to be relevant to this life experience, then it mutes the information; it lets it go, kind of like a butterfly fluttering about in the garden. The butterfly is part of the whole landscape, the flowers and trees, the air and soil, the other insects, and animals; it is part of it all. Pretend there is a net, a garden net, that stays in the garden. It captures the butterfly, and it stays in the garden with the butterfly in it. The butterfly went from being part of the lush landscape—seeing everything it could see, touching and feeling all the elements—to an extremely limited environment. The butterfly, when it got caught in the net, forgot the outer landscape to focus on its current environment inside the net.

A butterfly net, as you know, has holes. (They are not very big holes in our garden net because we do not want the butterfly's wings to get caught and hurt.) The thing about the net, though, is that it remains in the garden; it has not actually removed the butterfly from the landscape. It has temporarily hampered its view. If the butterfly were to shift its nearsighted focus to a farsighted one, it might see through the holes of the net it is in and catch glimpses of the broader landscape.

Thinking of the garden and meadows surrounding it, with wheat bowing in the breeze, and the butterfly net, let us once again go back to the kitchen and make pasta water.

The kitchen is its own environment. It has air, countertops, a stove, an oven, refrigerator, sink, pots, pans, and utensils. We can add a window or two as well. To make pasta, we are going to fill a pot about halfway with water. Bring it to a boil and add the pasta. Cook the pasta for three to five minutes if it's fresh, and maybe ten to twelve minutes if it's dried.

While the pasta is cooking, put a glass bowl into the sink, and put a white colander over the top. Once the pasta is ready, take it to the sink and pour the water and pasta into the colander. The water is going to collect in the glass bowl. If we'd dumped the pasta and water into the glass bowl directly, it would have splattered the water out of the bowl, with the pasta going everywhere, and it would just be a mess.

The colander catches the information coming from the pot. It says, "Okay, this is all familiar. But this pasta doesn't belong in the glass bowl. It's not relevant to the glass bowl, but the water is."

Now the water, once it's in the glass bowl in the sink, has a very limited point of view of the kitchen. The sink is all white, as is everything around it. Even the colander holding the pasta and the ceiling above that are white. But we, the makers of the pasta water, can see it all. We can put it into perspective; we can see how it's all connected and how it all works together.

Your mind is like the colander, capturing familiar frequencies, and your brain is like the bowl, translating the relevant information into your life. Sometimes bits of pasta get through the holes of the colander and enter the bowl with the water. At first it looks like the pasta bits belong there, that they are relevant to the pasta water, but if you just wait a few minutes, the pasta bits will settle to the bottom and will not be used by the water.

An example of information passing through our veil system that is not relevant to this life experience may be seen in some children remembering different life experiences, commonly referred to as "past life" memories. These past lives are music notes in our symphony because parts of the note look familiar to our net, and the snippets may get through to the brain. But, once the brain understands the information to be irrelevant, the memories fade, or they might even turn off, like a light switch. Interestingly, some children remember life experiences that have yet to happen upon this earthbound timeline; they remember future life experiences instead of past life experiences. It is hard to differentiate those examples from childhood play, though, because we cannot fact-check as we can with past life memory. We usually regard the future memories as a child having a great imagination. And like the past-life memory, the brain will eventually quiet the future-life memories because they are not relevant in the child's current life.

How are we obtaining our knowledge? In my book *Inside Past-Life Connections*, I touched on how we obtain our knowledge, that we obtain information from our overarching consciousness into this life rather than from this life into our consciousness. The keys are observation, interaction, and comprehension. One of the very first things we do upon our birth is to initiate a form of communication. Communication helps with survival and is usually a cry, and as we cry, we begin to understand that it equals a result. The more we practice our cry, the more we'll begin to know how it relates to our life and survival.

Once this comprehension is in place, the pathways between your consciousness and your brain adjust to your surroundings; the initial cry will no longer be relevant once you increase the range of your cries, a different cry for different needs. As you grow, you'll observe, watch, interact with, and implement new forms of communication. Communication, whether silent or vocal, is essential.

When I talk about pathways connecting earthbound life to the ethereal, I am not talking about the synapses we observe in the brain. I use the word "pathways" as symbolism. When I talk about them, I am just using an image to put along with a form of "quantum entanglement" (not necessarily an accurate image—we are using that infamous grain of salt). While the pathways are not really like a wire or thread connecting two points, with information running up and down it, that image is an idea we can grasp. The interesting thing about the phenomenon of quantum entanglement is that scientists say two subatomic particles can be intimately linked to each other even if separated by billions of light-years of space, across dimensions, and even across universal planes. Despite their vast separation, a change induced in one particle will affect the other. What they are observing, though, is not two subatomic particles; they are observing a form of "quantum superposition," where a particle can be in multiple places simultaneously. The quantum world is not segregated by theory or hypothesis; it is fluid and intertwined, and mathematics only touches a fraction of this world. Scientists set up experiments to prove or find an answer to a specific question or series of questions. By doing this, they isolate a tiny fraction of the natural activity of the quantum world into something observable, something understandable.

Imagine a beautiful Persian rug, where each thread knots and weaves together, creating a story where every knot affects the other, whether they are directly touching or thousands of knots away. When we look at the subatomic world, no matter how in-depth the experiment may be, it is really only looking at a single knot on a palace-size tapestry that has over one thousand knots per square inch. Then, the experimenter takes the observation of the single knot and explains the entire design and intricacies of the whole tapestry. In reality, we have no idea what went into the tapestry, how it formed, what it looks like, how it is affected by the measurements of observation, or anything, really.

The good thing is that nature loves patterns. They might be disordered patterns, but they are patterns all the same. The human brain contains an estimated 86 billion neurons. Scientists have discovered more than sixty distinct types of neurotransmitters in the human brain, with many more still to be discovered. Neurotransmitters are multifaceted and complex, working both with each other and against each other to aid in neural signaling across the brain's cortex. Your brain is demodulating information from your mind. Your mind is an external part of the filtration system of your consciousness and swirls in and above your brain. Your brain houses subatomic particles that are "superimposed" (in the quantum sense) both inside and outside the skull. They are subatomic particles of our consciousness. This is something that has not yet been observed in the lab or through experiments and does not work exactly like the experiments of quantum superposition have shown.

This phenomenon is an alternate version of a similar phenomenon because it works outside the realms of physical observation and measurement.

Once outside the veil, there is no measurement of time, meaning we are inside our consciousness, and the particles superimposed are one and the same. There is no distance. Our consciousness houses all information, ethereal and earthbound, outside the human brain. When a stimulus comes through the filter of the mind, the brain sets off a series of activities that turns on or off or opens and closes signals, neural responses that correlate to the vibrational code received. The brain can house temporary memory. We can see this activity when monitoring the brain.

When we, in our life here on earth, are ready for more information, or if there is information that is no longer needed, our brains adjust, and we try to act in accordance with this particular life experience.

In the background, of course, your brain also monitors and oversees your body's mechanical workings: heart, lungs, liver, kidney, stomach, etc. We do not need to think about these processes or regulate them. We only really notice these processes when a malfunction occurs. If we try to alter their working, it sets off a little bit of chaos, much like trying to straighten vibration. When you do this, you end up stopping it, and turning a wave into a flat line. The human body works without us having to think about it, and our bodies know what to do and how to do it. Again, we only really notice the processes of our bodies when an alteration to their norm occurs.

The processes of your body work in a form of disordered order. Like the developing disorder of our cream and tea nebula, your brain and body also work in a similar fashion. Think of the theory or principle of least action, briefly mentioned earlier, where the distribution of resources is optimized in an instantaneous calculation beyond that of trial and error. Part of this calculation happens by taking the kinetic energy of the particle and subtracting the potential energy, then integrating this result over the path of the particle:

Time Integral over

Kinetic Energy

minus Potential Energy

is the Action of the Particle:

$S = \int (T - V) \, dt$

where:

S represents the action of the particle,

T represents the kinetic energy of the particle,

V represents the potential energy of the particle,

$\int$ indicates the integration over time, and

dt represents an infinitesimal element of time.

In this equation, the action is given by the integral of the difference between the kinetic energy (T) and the potential energy (V) of the particle with respect to time (dt). The action is a fundamental concept in physics and plays a significant role in various areas, such as classical mechanics and quantum mechanics.

To obtain the action that has the smallest possible value, we can either make the kinetic energy small, which means keeping the velocity small, or we can make the potential energy large, because that enters the equation with a negative. In other words, when we make the potential energy larger, that larger potential energy is being subtracted immediately from the kinetic energy. The subtraction sign is in front of the potential energy (minus potential energy) when it enters the equation. This means, essentially, that the particle tries all possible paths, all happening instantly.

When we feel like we are working on making a decision, the decision is already made before we are aware we have a "choice." I've put "choice" in quotes because our overarching consciousness is observing both sides of the choice. It is looking at what happens from going down each of those trajectories. Only it is not pondering the choice as we do. It is observing the whole, all sides, and all variants.

When we try to play out our choices and weigh out their different sides, we think we are picking sides. This process can make us sick, meaning it can make us anxious, pace the floor, and lose sleep. We stress over what we think the outcome will be. We have expectations of what we think should happen, but we do not get to force those expectations into being. We cannot control what happens on any side of the choices, no matter how wise we think they are, no matter how much research we have done. The only thing we can control (to a point) is our behavior. When making the decision, all we have to look at is how we will react or respond to the sides of the choice. When we know what our behavior is, then we can move into this choice with more confidence and understanding.

And that is what happens in nature. A particle does not just go on one seemingly optimal path. It actually goes on all paths, and each of these paths has its own action. Not only does the particle travel all paths; it also travels to all possible endpoints.

Let us say you were to observe the particle (which is measuring the particle). In order to do this, a "wave function" collapses. A wave function is a fundamental concept in quantum mechanics that describes the state of a quantum system. We need to remember that when we measure or describe things such as we do in the quantum realm, we add limitations, parameters for the theory to fit within so we can turn it into something we can understand or describe. In the case of wave functions, they are considered a mathematical function that encodes information about the probability distribution of different possible outcomes when we measure the system. The wave function represents the probability amplitude associated with each possible state of the system. The particle you observe as part of this wave function only exists in one point.

When we observe our life experience from this human body, this is what we are doing. We are collapsing wave functions to see points. The points we are observing expose probabilities/possibilities for our human particle. We can pretend the possibilities are like potential energy.

Right now, as we are experiencing life, we sometimes feel like we're living in the twilight zone, where moments of our days feel more like dreams than reality. Where our earthbound life is more of a hologram, and the ethereal side is more real. We are holograms. We are comprised of vibrating molecules. If we were to place our hand beneath a super-high-powered microscope, the microscope could zoom through the kaleidoscope of cells, and atoms, and molecules until it zooms all the way through our hand to the other side. Scientists are exploring this form of technology in the medical field. A team in Seoul, South Korea, at the Center for Molecular Spectroscopy and Dynamics within the Institute of Basic Science (IBS) developed a reflection matrix microscope capable of imaging through bone.

The concept that life could be a hologram is rooted in certain theoretical frameworks and ideas from physics, particularly in the context of quantum mechanics and the holographic principle. It is important to note that this is a speculative idea and is still the subject of ongoing scientific debate and exploration.

In quantum theory, the holographic principle basically says that our three-dimensional reality might be a projection or illusion originating from a two-dimensional surface or "holographic screen" when applied to the observable universe. The idea is that all the information and physical laws governing our universe could be encoded on this boundary or third-dimensional plane, with the illusion of three-dimensional space emerging from it.

The quantum hologram theory could help explain certain things, like the smoothness of the cosmic microwave background radiation or the odd behavior of black holes. With the universe fundamentally being a hologram, it shows an underlying interconnectedness, which is fantastic because that is going to describe what is happening.

As we experience this life, we will look at our experience as potential energy; this is where all the possibilities of this life are pooled, so imagine a lake on top of a dam—let us say that is the potential energy. In this lake, our consciousness is observing, looking at all the possibilities, thinking, "I wonder what would happen if he went over there, but what if this happened, what if that happened, what if he came to this situation?" All those questions and their outcomes are being pooled into this lake of potential. Once all of that is done, the dam breaks, and all this water, all the possibilities, are released and become like kinetic energy or active energy. This is where our life becomes harmony. The lake of possibilities creates the musical note at the same moment the dam breaks (when the body ceases—not a near-death experience, but when the last leaf falls, per se). The musical note is a compilation of all observed possibilities. The creation of this musical note happens outside the third dimension and happens with the formation of the lake, otherwise considered the inception of you. Both the ceasing and creating of this particular life are fused. They are together and are inseparable. With the creating and ceasing of the lake of potential, the kinetic musical note flows into the ribbon of our overarching consciousness, the conscious symphony.

On another scale, this pool of possibilities is at work regarding our body and brain calibration. Our brains take all stimuli, observe all potentials that stimulus could mean, and instantly adjust. If we were to slow the process of possibility to a point that we could see it, it would look disordered. Not just the brain functions within the disorder, but the entire body. Every organ and every nerve works; they are all making a cream and tea nebula.

With this idea in mind, we can see how it correlates with our three-dimensional life, where our consciousness is instantly processing or observing all possibilities this life has—not just our choices but also the environment and our interaction with it. The workings of nature in this way result in running efficiently and with minimal effort, forming harmony.

The reason we experience our life as we do is because we are the thought process of our consciousness. We are not a noun; we are not a thing. We are inside the stream of consciousness; we are the stream of consciousness.

The Vantage Points of Isolation

Back to the kitchen.

The smell of baking cookies fills the air and fills my heart with savory temptation. My mouth can feel the warm texture, the smooth, creamy melted chocolate, the buttery vanilla, the crisp exterior, the soft interior… I wait a few more seconds, then, holding the hot pad, I open the oven door, take hold of the 375-degree baking sheet, and transfer it to a cooling rack. Warm, beautiful golden disks rest before me, dotted with dark chocolatey mountains. It is almost all one can bear...

While waiting for them to cool, let us look at one of the cookies. From where I am standing, the cookie is still on the baking sheet. I cannot see the bottom of the cookie or the lower far edge of the cookie. I cannot see inside the cookie.

I want to see inside the cookie, though, and I want to see the bottom of the cookie, so I use my thin metal spatula and slide it under the tempting crust. I use my hand to take the cookie and turn it over. The bottom is a little darker than the top, but it is not burnt, thank goodness.

While it is turned over, I can no longer see the top; I cannot see all the edges or the parts that are below my fingers holding it. I really want to see the whole cookie, though, all of it, all at the same time. So I came up with an ingenious idea: the cookie camera. I got a camera lens with built-in lighting, one big enough to set my cookie on. I hooked it up to an external screen to look at the cookie in real time.

Once I had the cookie camera, my eyes could quickly shift from the top of the cookie to the bottom picture of the cookie displayed on the screen, which then got me wondering what the cookie looked like on the inside. I got a couple of very tiny cameras that could go into the cookie: one from the bottom and one from the top.

I can now see what the inside looks like just above the bottom, and I can see what it looks like just underneath the top crust.

As I do this, I notice I cannot really see the whole thing from either angle. There are mountains of chocolate chips, and there are granular elements in the way. To get the details I'm after, I get a few more of these tiny cameras and set them up. I get a lot more because I keep finding that no matter where I put the cameras, there are always places I cannot see.

My external monitor is broken up into a kaleidoscope of images. At this point, I have lots of cameras, one for every grain of cookie, and tiny cameras to look at all sides of every single grain of the cookie. There are so many images that my eyes dart from one to another, still not seeing the whole cookie simultaneously. My eyes might be able to see the screen filled with millions of pictures, but my brain cannot comprehend all of them at the same time, even though they are all there. Except, of course, I did not get quite enough cameras to look inside the grains and into the molecules. That would be going a little overboard, and I needed to draw a line in the sand somewhere so my observations would not just keep going into perpetuity.

Trying to see the whole cookie at the exact same time, I enlisted the help of a friend who specializes in 3D models, and he made one of the cookies using all the information I had gathered. Now I could use the computer to spin the cookie, tilt it at different angles, and look inside from any vantage point. The model was impressively lifelike.

There was only one problem with it.

With the computer model, not only could I not see the whole cookie at the same time, but I also could not taste, smell, or feel the cookie. So I returned to the kitchen where the cookie was and went back to the drawing board, thinking, "I am not so different from this cookie."

At our inception, a particle is created with its very own genetic code, one that is entirely unique from any other. Your energetic footprint is just as unique. This idea is important, because when you interact with other people, beings, plants, and animals, this energetic code is what radiates from your body, describing who and what you are, what you look like, and everything else. The translation of that information forms a material image, whether that image is sound, taste, smell, feel, or sight. All those senses are waves that your brain translates into a form of materialization, a hologram of sorts. The brain reads this information on the ethereal plane, but on that plane, we do not have form. We remain in a kind of "wave state." I say a wave state because a wave is a form of measurement that we have devised with our 3D brains to describe something. Outside that 3D lens, however, things are far different. There is no time.

Let's take a moment to look at a little quantum physics. Scientists have demonstrated that particles can exist in multiple places simultaneously. But that's not all. Since every particle or group of particles in the universe is also a wave, waves can occupy multiple spaces at once. That means that since we are both a wave and a particle in observation, we can also do this. And waves occupy multiple positions in space at once, so any chunk of matter can also occupy multiple places at once. The material reality that you experience before your body ceases occurs through observation. Without observation, your particular life experience would not exist in the "material" state you are in now...

As far as we can tell, humans can only see about 4.9 percent of the matter comprising the observable universe. The rest is an approximate combination of dark matter (at about 26.8 percent) and dark energy (at 68.3 percent). We cannot see dark energy or dark matter, which are entirely unknown to us at this time; some scientists have started to calculate gravity's relation to such material, but again, we need to take such calculations with a grain of salt. The observable universe includes large particles, bacteria, trees, animals, rocks, planets, stars, dark matter, dark energy, antimatter, and, interestingly enough, human beings.

The observation of our life is a form of

quantum superposition. Scientists are beginning to witness, as reported in the *Journal of Nature Physics*, that groups of molecules, up to two thousand atoms, can occupy two places simultaneously.

In 1978, at six years old, I hid the following letter in the forest, buried in a glass jar—a letter to myself sent via the Flower Lady.

Dear Flower Lady,

Last night the light came again. It sat on the bed with me so I could sleep. And then light showed me my whole life. It flashed just like it does when I meet people. All my whole life flashed right in front of my heart almost. It was outside my heart, but I was inside it. I was like a tree. I could stretch through my branches. I could wiggle my twigs. I was inside the tree and outside the tree watching all of it. I was each branch. I was not different on each branch, each branch was just me

doing something different. Like each branch was each side of a choice. I was in all the choices at the same time. It was like I was a shoelace. I weaved back and forth in the shoe, and I was both the left side and the right side of the bow because I was the exact same lace. It was like standing on the teeter-totter. My right foot on one side and my other foot on the other side. And I balanced it. Is that what is happening? Are we balancing a life? Is that why things feel lopsided sometimes? I think I am in two places at the same time. I think I am in more than two places at the same time. Can you send a message to me for me? Today is my birthday. I got to pick my cake. A yellow cake with chocolate frosting or a grasshopper pie. It was a hard choice. I picked the grasshopper pie and the me you are sending this to picked the yellow cake with chocolate frosting. Now I am going to be having two

different kinds of life because of that. I think it is the teeter-totter. The different kinds of life are going to balance me. Like if I stub my toe, I won't stub my toe, either. Just tell myself on the yellow cake choice, I am not alone because I am here. Maybe I will sleep better knowing this.

Dreaming of cake,

Me

Let's pretend our particle is the epicenter—kind of like an observation tower for a sentry, who is a part of our symphonic consciousness on the other side of the veil. Our sentry's job is to observe every potentiality of this life, of this unique DNA code, so there is a lot to observe. There are many possible outcomes of this life, and if our observation tower has only one window to look out of, then our sentry cannot observe them all. For this reason, our watch tower is fitted with millions of windows. Each window shows a potential outcome of the life created, which allows our sentry to observe each one of these trajectories without confusion or interference from the others. Each vantage point is isolated from the others. Having multiple vantage points for observation trajectories creates a duality (well, a multi-ality: a duality of a duality of a duality...). Each possibility of this life has its own trajectory, starting from the observation tower. Each trajectory is in isolation. The isolation for each one of these potential outcomes helps our observation balance.

Experiences in life create variables. Our choices—for example, on how we react and respond to life's internal and external environmental interactions—create independent variables. These independent variables change the angle of the observation trajectory.

Life weaves together, carefully. All the experiences create neutrality, which creates balance and harmonization, thus making this life experience whole, total, and complete. This particular life experience cannot be replicated through any other DNA code, even if it were your clone, because performing this life experience starting with conception on different days or at various times (even with a micro-millisecond difference) would cause unrepeatable variation due to the unique differences in just that mere flicker of time and would yield different results.

Conception has a set of conditions that maximizes the power to analyze the effects of changes in variables for that particular code. The baseline for observation is our unique particle, and from there, through environmental experiences, our ethereal consciousness's (our sentry's) observation takes place while always keeping our particle constant, which includes both sides of our choices, our reactions, and responses to situations that change the trajectory.

Right now, as we experience this life, life is potential energy where all its possibilities are pooled, like a lake above a dam, gathering an arrangement of possible movements. When the human body ceases, our kinetic energy is realized through the breaking of the dam, where our life's specific musical note flows into the ribbon of our overarching symphony/consciousness.

Bubbles, Goldilocks, and the Three Bears

The temperature was below freezing, the sun low on the horizon; the air was still, as were the birds. My feet crunched over and through the frozen snow, and in my gloved hands I held my camera, sugared bubble solution, and a straw. On the edge of the forest, I set my camera down, then turned it on to film directly in front of it. Then I opened the solution, dipped the end of my straw in, and blew several bubbles. Carefully.

I filmed the bubbles freezing. Crystalizing patterns grew, some like fern leaves in the spring, others like snowflakes dancing and joining together. Eventually, no matter the pattern, the crystals grew, branching, spreading, and weaving together, creating a breathtaking orb.

Our lives are breathtaking; they form through their own unique vibration, creating crystalline structures that develop (in this case) from the orb created by the bubble solution, the straw, and the interacting environments, from both inside and outside the sphere.

When watching the crystals develop and spread, I noticed that some had long, graceful movements like a vein running through the center to the smaller and shorter branching of fern leaves. The beauty created by this combination is surreal. Our lives play out in this same way; the possibilities are the crystal structure forming on the bubble. The one constant we have in our particular life experience is our inception. We cannot change the inception point that creates our particle because any deviation from that and the perspective would be altered, and we would not be who we are. We would be a different life experience completely.

It does not matter if some of our observational trajectories of this life experience finish as children or as young adults or all the way to 108 years old. Time works differently on ethereal planes than it does on this earthbound one. The trajectory that was completed moments after conception, or was miscarried or aborted or had a childhood illness, and the trajectory that was completed at 108 years old finished simultaneously, as they are the exact same particle. They finished with our inception and death.

A question that often arises at this point is, does that cycle go on forever? Do the possibilities of this particular life observation go on indefinitely? They go on for quite a bit, for sure, because there are innumerable branches of each primary trajectory of possibility, but our bodies are designed in such a way that they do not last forever. They have a form like the soap bubble did. Our bodies are made of organic material and have a limited life span and are made to age and decompose, just like any other material. The rate of decomposition and how that looks is different to each form. Even granite undergoes a process of decomposition through weathering, chemical, and biological reactions over extended periods of time. Life here is not meant to last forever; it is all made to alter and end in some way, shape, or form.

This situation helps take the duality of our life experience and translate it into a form of nonduality, where all the observed potentialities of this life harmonize when this body ends, and all the potential paths balance one another and create a magnificent crystal, a vibrational note.

Our crystal patterns are unique to each of us and form from the fluid vibrational movement of our musical notes: the notes that were created at our conception. I use music notes as a representation of size in comparison to our overarching symphony, where inside our music note is a symphony itself, where the melody is our life's signature frequency. And all the potential pathways fluidly forming the crystals are the tones and pitches, the flats and sharps, the color and quiet of our personal symphony that makes up this single note, which is full and complete.

When we play with the idea of a multiplicity of duality, we create underlying balance in the form of a whole. This balance then creates neutrality, which in turn creates harmony.

A simple look at duality and nonduality

working together may be found in this abridged story of the Three Bears, with Mama Bear, Papa Bear, and Baby Bear being the dual and nondual elements. When Goldilocks tries the porridge from Papa Bear's bowl, it is too hot, and Mama Bear's is too cold, but when combined to create Baby Bear's porridge, she finds that it's just right. Baby Bear's porridge is balanced. It is neutral. It harmonizes both the hot and cold, which is what Goldilocks enjoyed—she enjoyed the "balance."

We can pretend that Goldilocks is like us, our observational consciousness. She tastes, observes, and experiences Papa Bear's hot porridge; the inverse, which is Mama Bear's cold porridge; and the in between or blend of the two, which is Baby Bear's "just right" porridge. In terms of duality and nonduality, we can pretend that the hot and cold porridge make up dual states of the porridge, and the just-right porridge is the nondual state. In order to attain the nondual state, however, we need to combine the duality. And in order for the nonduality state of the porridge to remain just right, the states of duality, the hot and cold porridge, must remain as well. Here's an equation, where "DS" = "dual state":

Porridge 1 Dual State + Porridge 2 Dual State = (P1DS + P2DS) = P3DS

(Mama Bear) + (Papa Bear) = (Baby Bear)

Then we take (P1DS + P2DS) = P3DS and divide it by P3DS, which leads to 1, or the nonduality we will call the "Goldilocks Porridge State." Without one of the dual states, there is no nonduality, nor is there any duality.

Because we are playing out every side to every situation, multiples of this equation happen at all times. In addition, as part of our completed life experience, these variants of the equation blend between themselves as dualities and nondualities. Here's another equation:

Goldilocks Porridge 1 Dual State + Goldilocks Porridge 2 Dual State = ([GP1DS + GP2DS] = GP3DS) / GP3PS or the Goldilocks Porridge State: 1 or the nonduality

This Goldilocks Porridge State works with another Goldilocks Porridge State, creating another Goldilocks Porridge State or nondual combination. We can also change the word "Goldilocks" to "Life Trajectory" and get:

Life Trajectory State A + Life Trajectory State B = ([LTSA + LTSB] = LTSAB) / LTSAB = 1 or nondual state

The initial variants may make the porridge taste a little hotter or colder (or a life trajectory more turbulent or calm), depending on the blend. But when each of those combinations moves into other combinations, things arise that look like nebulas as they flow into dualities and nondualities of their own, eventually finding an equilibrium. If you were inside this process, inside this nebula, then you'd find it to be like swimming in the middle of the ocean. If you were there, in the middle of the ocean, treading water, would you be able to see the entirety of the ocean, all the storms and shorelines, the calm seas and the very bottom, across all of the ocean?

In our lives, we experience a multitude of both dual states and nondual states. Just like nature (because we are nature), we cannot have one without the other. We cannot have the top of a piece of paper without a bottom. Nor can we have a top and bottom without the sides. And to get to the side, we'll first encounter an in-between. This same idea goes for inside and outside, positive and negative, separate and together, up and down, etc. We cannot have a long trajectory of this life experience without a short one. We cannot have a wild trajectory without a calm one.

In the story of the Three Bears, Goldilocks

was still Goldilocks, even after she'd tasted each porridge; she tasted all the porridge from her unique vantage point, and she did not turn into anyone else before each taste. For her to savor Baby Bear's porridge, she needed the others. She needed to experience them, not take someone else's word for them, or eat one porridge, die, come back as someone else to eat the next, die, and come back again to taste the last one as someone else.

If that happened, she would not have the chance to know Baby Bear's porridge or Mama Bear's because she would not be the same Goldilocks. Her unique vantage point would change after each death, and she could never come back as the same Goldilocks who had tasted Papa Bear's porridge. All three of these "Goldilocks" lives would be incomplete. Like Goldilocks, we experience and observe all possibilities as ourselves. And when this life experience ceases, we become a music note in the symphony.

Becoming a harmonious musical note may not sound like much, but it is an important part of the grand symphony. Our music is a movement where each note plays within a continuous spectrum, harmonizing this life experience into a musical phenomenon that facilitates performance, comprehension, and analysis. The idea of an angelic choir is a small representation of ethereal music. The choir is part of something greater than humility, greater than love, and greater than the deepest compassion.

Part 2—Questions

Brain Waves and the End of Life

How would everything we've discussed so far affect manifesting and raising your vibration or your frequency?

We are electromagnetic organisms, and we work within an optimal range or band of frequency. As discussed earlier, frequency is the number of times a wave repeats itself per second. The human brain has multiple frequencies that are always playing. These frequencies distribute harmonic patterns, depending on the interacting stimulus signatures. The harmonic distribution is generalized across different states of functional consciousness. Our mental activity can be affected if any of these frequencies are overabundant, deficient, or just difficult to access.

You may have heard the term "raising our frequencies" to connect to the other side of the veil. Before we look at that idea in more detail, let us first see what these frequency ranges are through a test that detects the electrical activity of your brain (an electroencephalogram, or EEG). Brain waves are usually described in terms of frequency bands, including gamma (greater than 30 Hz), beta (13–30 Hz), alpha (8–12 Hz), theta (4–8 Hz), and delta (less than 4 Hz).

Gamma is usually very localized and works

between 30–44 Hz but can go all the way up to 100 Hz in bursts. In this range of frequency, you might integrate thoughts, access memories, or consolidate areas for simultaneous processing, hyperfocused on information processing. This is more of an acute state of mind: you are hypervigilant, in a real state of fight or flight. You are ready for anything. This is also a place where your Ferris wheel of memory goes around, and around, and around. If we are in this state too long, we can experience anxiety and irritation.

Beta has a frequency range between 13–30Hz. This activity is fast. This range is generally regarded as a normal rhythm, and the higher-range beta waves are dominant when we need to be alert or if we are anxious, but throughout the day we usually spend time in a lower and sometimes midrange band of beta. Our eyes are open and are listening, problem-solving, making decisions, and processing what is happening in our environment. We are fully engaged at this point and would really not be comfortable sitting and reading a novel. We use this frequency to pay attention when driving in hazardous conditions or cooking a new recipe that we don't want to mess up. In higher-range beta, your brain tends to jump from ideas and distractions to planning, learning, and processing. When we are in a high beta state, we can feel more agitated with a prolonged stay.

Alpha works in a range of 8–12 Hz and is where we find keen resourcefulness and mental coordination. You are alert, still engaged with the world around you, and can move around easily to get your work done, and you usually feel relaxed and calm. Alpha is one of the brain's most important frequencies to learn and is a great state to be in while reading a book.

Theta (4–8 Hz) is for daydreaming. In this band, intuition seems a little louder and creativity flows; fantasy, memories, and spiritual awareness all seem to dwell in the land of theta. At least, this is the state that quiets the noise of the world just enough to feel the theta waves. If you are reading a book in this state, you enter the pages and might wander beyond the words as your brain makes up the in-between. Theta bridges your wakefulness and sleep and is believed to reflect activity from the limbic system and hippocampal regions. Delineating what is real and what is not real is difficult when we engage in a dream state. Your book falls onto your lap, and you are completely relaxed; your eyes begin to close, and you drift into the delta.

The delta—ah, your eyes are closed in this wonderfully low-frequency band of 0.1–3.5 Hz. Just as the term "sleep like a baby" implies, infants up to about a year of age spend most of their time rocking in the slow waves of the delta. Delta has the highest amplitude and is found in our deep, dreamless sleep, the non-REM sleep. We enter the delta band in a trance, which decreases our awareness of the physical world; in delta, we enter the unconscious earthbound state.

These bands of energy help modulate or regulate what is going on with your body physically. The body naturally moves in and out of these frequencies, and the brain tailors them. Let's say that we're in alpha and we want to raise this vibrational frequency; we want to get it up into that high beta band of about 25–30 Hertz. Turn a light switch on, stand up and shake around, do a few small jumps, yawn, and get your brain engaged. You are going to heighten your awareness of everything around you and focus intently on your task. How long you stay in this state depends on you. We can practice moving into states and working in them, which might help to create a little endurance. But your brain is not meant to stay in one state or another for extended periods; it naturally moves between them. So if you are focused intently on something, after a while, you might start to feel woozy, hungry, or agitated. These are ways that your brain says, "It's time to change our position; we need a break."

Going into gamma mode is not meant to be a state of endurance. We enter it for specific tasks and memory recall. We've seen this gamma state turn on when the rest of the brain waves subside just prior to death. While pinpointing the exact last brain activity before death is difficult, a phenomenon known as "terminal lucidity" has been reported in some cases. Terminal lucidity refers to a brief period when the gamma waves ignite, which creates a form of mental clarity and consciousness that occurs shortly before death. Interestingly, it also occurs in patients with severe cognitive impairments or neurological disorders. The exact cause of terminal lucidity is still not well understood in the medical and scientific fields.

Knowing that this end-of-life clarity happens no matter if the brain has impairments or not helps to show that the consciousness outside the body is viable, that impairments or impediments are earthbound and are only part of the physical body. They do not carry over or continue after this body ceases.

In the last moments of life, general brain activity declines due to lack of oxygen and nutrient supply. This decline happens as the body's systems begin to shut down. The exact sequence of events and the last specific activity may vary, depending on the cause of death, individual differences, and other factors. But the gamma waves can continue for a short time after death, which contributes to the memory associated with near-death experiences. The increase of gamma activity happens whether the death is sudden or prolonged. The brain being in the final gamma state incites what many people say is a "life review." This life review occurs as part of the earthbound experience, not in the ethereal.

"Raising Your Vibration"

As we have discussed, the body works on frequency. Your personal frequency signature shares the minute details of your body, how you are feeling, all the way to your intentions with the world around you. Your frequency signature is like a fingerprint. If you put a fingerprint on a board, we could say, generalizing, "Okay, that's a human fingerprint." But when we look closer at that fingerprint, we find it is unique unto its own. If you put your frequency on a board, you could do the same thing: generalize that the frequency signature is human. Then, as we delve further, we will see that each frequency, too, is unique unto its own, just like the fingerprint. When we look at the frequencies of the human body, specifically the brain, we can see that it has an optimal range of functioning. There is an optimal range of functioning in each band and as a whole, containing all bands. The brain modulates in and out of gamma, beta, alpha, theta, and delta throughout the day, according to what's going on in the body or in the environment around the body.

Many people have been told that they must raise their frequency to alter their connection with their intuition and their consciousness. The frequencies discussed above help the physical body optimize its functionality, depending on its environment and needs.

Raising vibration is not what connects us

to our consciousness. We want to shift away from that idea and take a closer look at harmony and resonance. They are related concepts but have different contexts with distinct meanings. Let's examine the definitions and differences between the two.

Harmony

In music, harmony refers to the simultaneous combination of different musical notes or chords to create a pleasing or consonant sound. It is an essential aspect of music composition, where individual notes are combined to create a rich, layered, and expressive sound. Harmony adds depth and complexity to a musical piece, creating tension and resolution, both of which contribute to the emotional impact of the music.

In nature, harmony is the weaving of elements, the weaving of our environment. It does not mean perfection. Harmony creates depth. It layers our connections by concurrently lacing us all together. It is the touch of sun upon your shoulders, upon the leaves, and upon the lakes; it is the rays that drift below the surface into the deep abyss, where light inverses and becomes the darkest of dark. It is the deep earth, where the springs of this depth encourage life, both in its darkness and upon the lighted surface.

Harmony combines these different vibrations concordantly. We are part of this harmony: we can feel it, we can taste it, we can experience it.

Resonance

Resonance is a physical phenomenon that occurs when an object or system is subjected to an oscillating force that matches its natural frequency, resulting in an increase in amplitude. In other words, resonance happens when a vibrating object causes another object to vibrate at the same frequency, amplifying the vibration. Resonance can be observed in various fields, such as physics, acoustics, and engineering.

Spiritually, resonance is what I believe most people are looking for when considering "raising their vibrations." Resonance plays a role in the amplification and projection of our ethereal vibration and connection. Like a guitar, our natural frequencies allow the vibration of conscious connection to feel fuller and deeper.

Both harmony and resonance are important to us. They complement one another; they complement our lives, and each serves different purposes that are not interchangeable.

When we talk about raising our vibrational frequency or raising our vibration, we're automatically assuming that we are taking a jump up and going higher, because we assume that our consciousness or "higher self" is above us. In order to reach that place above, we must raise our frequency, or maybe we need to raise our frequency to break through the ceiling, to break through the veil's barrier—think of a very high note that can break a glass vase.

Taking the term "raise my frequency" seriously would be like asking you to eat a bag of espresso beans on an empty stomach. A prolonged stay at a higher frequency will make you feel very, very agitated and uncomfortable and will eventually heighten your anxiety, because you're trying to go above your natural optimal range—a range that allows the body to fluctuate within its band in order to coincide with our interactions with the environment, both internal and external. Remember, these frequencies are for our physical body. They are not what dictates our connection to the ethereal, even though we often hear that raising our vibrational frequency will do that, or that this practice will allow you to connect with your higher self. But you're already awake. You're already fully engaged in something higher. We, you and me, are already connected to the ethereal, and nothing can break that.

What we want to say or what we want to do is find harmony and resonance. These two concepts are important to training our earthbound brain's relevance. They can help us feel and experience the ethereal connections we have.

When I was young, my brain longed to explore the unseen. At night I would venture further and further into the universe: not with a telescope or by looking at the heavens, but in my mind as my head rested on the pillow. At times, I felt the confines of this human body holding me back, and I wiggled my feet, felt the blankets, and made electrical storms under the sheets. The limitations of my body lasted mere moments before the cotton static lightning had me move into the lightning above the earth; that lightning then led me to the electrical beat of my heart, and soon I experienced a direct connection between how my body worked and the universe. Because of that connection, I wanted to touch the edge of the universe and look beyond it. To go further. Not in distance, not by space travel, because that would take too long; I might have run out of jet fuel and food, and this body would not last long enough to get there, let alone back. The power of resonance and harmony then played a pivotal role; the resonance of a hum allowed me into the ethereal harmony. Once in that harmony, I could go anywhere instantly; measurement did not exist, meaning that time did not exist. This combination allowed me into different vantage points of observation.

But was it the humming that facilitated this experience of exploration? Humming resonance is a good tool or marker to remind yourself of what it feels like to connect, to touch harmony. It offers a physical sensation that we can all feel, right where we are. Once we connect, we can incite that sensation without physically making sound. We can incite it at any moment of any day.

Using physical vibration to find this ethereal space is not a new idea; we naturally do it as children, and it has been a part of connected practices for many centuries. Think of the *om* (or *aum*) sound in Hinduism. When humming or practicing physical resonance, the body is reminded of this connection. The vibration is not aligning anything, though; you are not out of alignment. You do not want to be aligned, or even in a line at all—that is a narrowing of your resonance. Imagine taking a rubber band and strumming it, and you'll get that "boing" sound. Now, while it's making that sound, straighten it. You'll lose the vibration pretty quickly. This situation is like dropping a pebble on a frozen pond and expecting the ripple of fluidity.

Rather than looking for alignment, you want

to spread into the ethereal harmony, like melting ice cream on warm cement.

So, when I was young and I wanted this deep connection to wash over me, I would close my ears and my eyes, and I would begin humming. I would move the vibration from a shallow mouth sound to one that combined my abdomen, lungs, and head. (On a side note, you do not need to be a great singer; often while I tried to sing in the car, sitting next to my big sister, she'd tell me to stop because my singing voice was so bad—I still sang often in my head, though.) I would begin humming, I'd take a big breath from my abdomen, a four- to five-second inhale, and then I would hum with a consistent release that lasted up to a minute or so. I would play with the range of sound, moving it into something that made me feel there was no more body, no more delineation between my body and the interior and exterior world. Doing this melted the framework between here and there because neither one existed.

It moved me into ... nothing. But then, there can't be nothing without something. And so it goes, again, together, this vibrational dance of the ethereal.

In Hinduism, om is the means to hum. According to Indian philosophy, the om, or the syllable for om(ॐ), means the fundamental or the vocal manifestation of the Brahman (the ultimate reality or truth). Some also consider ॐ to be the all-encompassing essence of the universe.

When you start with your mouth open for the *O* or *au* sound—not separating the *a-u* into individual distinctions but vocalizing them as one—the vibration stays farther back in your throat. Other vowel sounds such as *e* and *i* push the vibration forward, away from your body. When you close your mouth, going from *o* into the *m* sound in a blending of the two, the vibration moves into the soft tissue of the back of the palate. You can adjust the pressure in your ears, sending the vibration into the marrow of your bones, vibrating it all from the core.

After you've played with this vibrational experience, your body may start to recognize similar dissolutions of earthbound and ethereal delineations without the need to physically hum. This situation is similar to meditation. Once your body knows the capability of meditation and humming, it can call upon them at any time, in any place.

Are Souls Eternal?

And do we reincarnate with the same group of spirits?

Yes, souls are eternal.

If we look at the soul as the musical note created by our overarching consciousness, our symphony, then we can understand that, as part of this symphony, the musical note does not just remain. It becomes. It becomes an integral part of the symphony. It houses memory and experience and resonates in the harmony of the symphony.

Reincarnation is an interesting topic on

its own. Our overarching consciousness observes many life experiences. Those life experiences are whole, total, and complete—just like this one. This particular life experience retains cognition beyond the body, but it does not morph into or transform into another life experience.

Here's another question: Do we pick our parents?

In a way, yes, although we are not making an agreement with them. Our overarching consciousness is a very curious thing, a little mischievous and creative. In the picking of parents, the decision occurs through the desire to observe a combination of two humans (or two animals or plants, or the type of asexual reproduction known as "parthenogenesis"—even the development of artificial intelligence, or AI). Our consciousness says, "I wonder what would happen with this combination; how would this combination react or respond to these situations?" Of course, I am simplifying this process with my own words.

When thinking of our overarching consciousness as a symphony—there are multiple symphonies, but we are part of a specific one, and that's what we're going to look at—our symphony can create another musical note. For this explanation, we'll look at human beings, but this idea applies to everything; even a tree is another musical note that our symphony can create. The symphony creates a unique particle when it brings two cells together, a sperm and an egg, and at inception, when that sperm breaks through the cellular wall of the egg, a magnificent event happens: an explosion, a firework of zinc, goes off when a human egg is activated. The life literally explodes into being, kind of like setting off our very own **Big Bang**. This is when our unique particle is created. Now, the energy of the physical sperm and the egg isn't new energy; it is recycled, just as everything we can observe is. The developing physical body uses energy from its surrounding. It initially uses the energy from the sperm and egg, which draw their energy from the bodies they came from. When they combine, they don't form just a physical form; this combination is the onset of a unique energetic code. The energetic code is what you might consider a soul.

This soul is unique. Its code is not replicated. It will not return to earth once it joins the symphony. At inception, a new signature of energy is created by combining two others. Now, once the life experience for that signature here on earth is done, two primary things happen. One, the organic body that we're housing right now and that we're moving around in goes back into the earth, whether we're buried or cremated. This material returns to this earthbound plane. Two, we have our beautiful ethereal code, the musical note, which goes into our symphony and remains part of that symphony.

Expressing Your Uniqueness

One question that people sometimes ask is: Do I need to express my uniqueness to the world through authentic creative expression for it to be seen? Among the most significant messages that nature tries to share is that we are enough just as we are. We don't need to be a certain somebody, and we don't need to look a certain way. We are not our jobs, and we are not what we wear. There's more to us than material goods. There's something much more special than what is on the outside. You're stunning, just as you are. There's nothing you need to do, and you don't have to try to prove that to anyone. There is no mission you are here to do, no unknown task for you to accomplish. Set your curiosity free, observe, and explore—even if it is in the smallest way. Feel the wind on the back of your hands if you want to draw or paint, sing or cry. All of that is exploration. When we are sad, each wave of sadness is its own wave. As relenting as those waves can be, space does exist between them. If we make mistakes, there is space between them. One of my favorite Flower Lady letters goes like this:

> **Dear Flower Lady,**
>
> **I think there may be a reason we cannot really see our own faces without a mirror. I believe we are not meant to focus on ourselves superficially. We are part of the canvas. When there isn't a mirror, we can walk into a room and forget ourselves,**

but with a mirror, people tend to fuss about their hair; they apologize for how they look..

They become a thing.

Imagine if mirrors were actually windows to the landscape outside, with the earth and trees, with the lunar moths and butterflies in the apple trees, with the rains and lightning, and the sun kissing the horizon. If that is what people saw in the mirror, they would feel beautiful..

There is a reason we don't see our own faces. Because we are already beautiful, we are already part of life..

Soul Agreements & Karma Carryover

People have spoken of reincarnation for thousands of years. According to one version of this idea, we recycle our lives to help those of our souls who have failed their earthly spiritual training, which is supposed to strengthen their enlightenment. When they fail to do so, they return to heaven to review their experiences and lessons learned (or not learned) with their soul group or soul family: usually six souls, including theirs. In that group there is a leader, or a core soul, which draws up a plan for reincarnation for each of the other souls. This plan gives the souls another chance to gain knowledge and increase their enlightenment.

Here is a simple story showing what this idea might look like.

Once upon a time, there was a little spirit in an apple. It was a lovely apple the little spirit lived in. The spirit in the apple grew up just outside town, in a small orchard with many other apples. Its apple life was full of apple experiences right from the very start.

After a cold winter's rest, the apple tree began to wake up. The budded branches began to unfold their leaves in the spring, and pink blossoms bloomed, one being the potential life of our little spirit in the apple.

Like the other apple buds, this one was sensitive to late-spring frosts. Honeybees were drawn to the flower by nectar and the beautiful light scent of its petals. When a bee landed on our little spirit's apple blossom, it brushed against the pistil, leaving pollen grains on the sticky stigma. The pollen grains reached the ovary, where the fertilized ovule became a seed.

Just by looking at the first few weeks of a pollinated ovule, an onlooker might say there's nothing special about it, not realizing that it's developing in such a way that the outer wall of the ovary will become the sweet, tender flesh of the apple, and the inner wall of the ovary will become its core, protecting the seeds.

Together with the other blooms busily working on their transformations on the apple tree, our little spirit's bloom helped brighten the quaint hillside.

In the summer, the little spirit's apple grew bigger and was soon touched by flies while laying their eggs, which grew into worms, which the birds pecked out. The apple gradually changed colors as it ripened in growth. In the fall, the little spirit's apple was picked.

A woman tasted the apple right off the tree, savoring its sweet and slightly tart flavor. She brought the apple into the kitchen, where she cored, sliced, and incorporated this apple, along with many other apples, into a myriad of dishes: a salad, applesauce, apple cider, everything you can imagine, except for one thing. It never became an apple pie.

Once the apple was all gone, the little spirit went up into the heavens to join other spirits. They all shared their many adventures and lives, and not all of them were apples. It was such a loving place to be. It was so much better than the apple tree. It was better than going home. It was a place of love—

beyond that, really.

One day as the spirits were talking and laughing and listening to music, a bigger spirit showed up. Its presence was like harmony itself.

The big spirit looked at our little spirit and spoke: "Looking over your files, I noticed you did not become an apple pie while you were on earth."

The little spirit nodded, confirming this.

The bigger spirit said gently but authoritatively, "You need to go back to earth and learn what it is to be an apple pie."

"Right now?" asked the little spirit.

"In a day or two. Head down there, and then you can come back up and will not have to go again because you will have learned your lesson. Does that not sound nice?" the big spirit said.

The little spirit nodded, trusting the wise big spirit.

A few days later, the little spirit went. This time the orchard was a little warmer than it had been before. The freezing winter was not as harsh. In fact, the winter season did not last long at all. Soon it was time to bloom.

The honeybees came by and pollinated the flowers, and the whole tree buzzed to life. The little petals fell as the fruits began to grow. For the little spirit, this was all new, because when it came back down to this tree, it came without remembering a thing that the big spirit had told it to do—it had no memory of even talking with the big spirit at all.

Life on this tree was hard.

There were so many diseases that the tree and fruits were constantly fighting. Some of the fruit went unscathed, and other fruits—well, they rotted right on the branch.

The little spirit went to one of the surviving fruits and asked, "What's going on? Did I do something to make my life so hard all the time? I feel so imbalanced. Something is missing. I don't know. I just don't know."

The other fruit spirit listened to the little spirit and said, "You are out of alignment. You did things in your past you have to make up for now. And you made a deal to learn these lessons before you came."

"What things?" the little spirit asked. "What can I do?"

The other fruit spirit sat quietly for a moment, then took a deep breath of the warm tropical air and said, "You made an agreement before you came to this tree. A spirit agreement. You chose to come down here and suffer."

The little spirit's heart sank. "Why would I do that? You mean, I asked for all this? I asked to be hurt, to be sick?"

"Well, yes. We all make agreements before coming down. Some agreements are to be in wonderful health, to be in that tree over there where there's no disease, no rot, no melanosis on the leaves. No sooty canker or mold. No rust. No greasy spots or scabs on their peels." The other fruit spirit continued, "Some of us have different agreements and lessons we need to learn. Some of us have a job to do, a mission."

"A mission?" asked the little spirit, with a little excitement.

"Yes, a mission," the other fruit spirit said.

"How do I know what I'm supposed to do? Or how do I know what I'm supposed to correct?" the little spirit inquired.

"There are several things you can do," the other fruit spirit said. "Recognize and accept the messages the universe sends your way. Also, practice self-awareness. Wait and listen for the answers."

After weeks of practicing mindfulness, reflecting, of taking responsibility for the diseases it had attracted to itself, the little spirit went back to the other fruit spirit and said, "I had an epiphany. I think I'm supposed to be an apple pie."

"That is wonderful," the other fruit spirit said. "It's going to take courage and a lot of work. But you can be the first orange ever to become an apple pie. And when you become an apple pie, that is when you will know peace."

What About Free Will?

Based on neuroscience and the concept of determinism, studies have shown that our brains make decisions before we are consciously aware of them, suggesting that our decisions are not truly the result of conscious choice but rather the product of neural activity that we are not aware of.

This concept shows hints at the brain using the principle of least action, which works with the idea of determinism. Determinism is a philosophical and scientific concept that suggests that all events, including human actions, are determined by prior causes or preexisting conditions, and therefore could not have happened in any other way.

The idea of determinism can be traced back to the ancient Greek philosophers, who believed in a kind of natural law that governed the behavior of the universe. Modern determinism is based on scientific theories, which suggest that every event has a cause, and that the outcome is determined by that cause.

There are several different types of determinism, including "hard" determinism—which holds that all human actions are determined by prior causes and that there is no such thing as free will—and "soft" determinism, which suggests that while human actions are influenced by prior causes, individuals still have some degree of choice and control over their behavior.

Determinism has been the subject of much

debate and discussion among philosophers and scientists, with some arguing that it is incompatible with the concept of free will.

We feel as though we have free will because we can physically feel our brains working when making certain decisions. The brain thinks and processes and finds a solution to the choice. We feel as though we are active participants in this process. But what about reactionary choices? We can have a reactionary choice that alters the course of our lives. Let's say you were attacked. Your body and brain went instantly into survival mode. Without having time to think, you reacted. In doing so, the attacker was harmed. Because of this reaction, you are sentenced to jail. You did not have time to think or deliberate in that situation; you acted instinctively. All the other choices you made in your life were well thought out, planned meticulously, to keep you on a solid path. How could one choice that you feel you did not make change it all? If we consider determinism, then all the well-thought-out choices and the deliberations would have led you right into the situation of being attacked.

If this is the case, then what prevents people from just behaving erratically or immorally? If we look at what morality is, we'll find a set of natural principles and values that guide human behavior and decision-making. While many people believe that morality is inherently linked to religion, moral codes originated without relying on religious beliefs.

Morality begins in our infancy: to communicate, we naturally use a form of empathy, which allows us to mimic our caregivers, including their expressions and compassion. Empathy is the ability to understand and share the feelings of others, while compassion is the desire to alleviate the suffering of others. By cultivating these qualities, people develop a sense of responsibility toward others and a desire to act in ways that will promote the well-being of others. Promoting the well-being of others helps to keep others safe and, in turn, keeps them safe. This survival mechanism leads to the development of a moral code that emphasizes the importance of treating others with kindness and respect and promotes values such as honesty, fairness, and social responsibility.

If someone behaves outside the moral code, they will be removed from the pack. This inherent reaction to danger stems from a focus on reason and rationality. Reason is the ability to think logically based on evidence and sound argumentation, while rationality is the ability to weigh the costs and benefits of different actions and then make choices that are in one's best interests. When we look at this rationality, where we weigh the costs of benefits of different actions, that is part of the disordered pool of potentialities we spoke of earlier, where we observe every side to every situation and choice we find ourselves in.

In developing a common morality, having a focus on social norms and cultural traditions has a substantial impact. Social norms are the unwritten rules that govern behavior in a particular society, while cultural traditions, the customs and practices passed down through generations, are a part of such norms. By learning and following these norms and traditions, people develop a sense of social responsibility and a commitment to maintaining the values and traditions of their community.

We are witnessing a push against moral codes in younger generations, who have the ability to use the power of social media and dating websites. The platforms have systemically shifted the importance of human connection to the importance of self. Instant gratification removes depth and development, which has had a direct and noticeable physical impact among young people. Rather than allowing their bodies the depth and development of all stages (uncomfortable as many of these stages are), they are pausing, stopping, and synthetically altering their body's natural development so they can feel instantly better. Only that is not what is happening. Long-term physical effects are taking root.

Rather than teaching people that there are wide spectrums of physical and personality traits in each gender code and that this is part of the beauty of our species, we teach them that they are not good enough as they are by telling them that nature got it wrong and that, for them to ever appreciate who they are, they must change. This is a superficial response to a deeper developmental situation. Doing this is like putting all the ingredients for stew into a pot and serving it right away, not allowing time for the stew's flavors to develop, the nuances of texture that come in at the various stages. No aromatic caramelization at the beginning to create the broth. As these elements in life unfold, they not only create connections for the individual but for society as well.

In the absence of free will, the inclination toward superficiality becomes an inherent aspect of the vast spectrum of possibilities. Free will is an integral part of the collective potential. I raise this matter to highlight the impact of societal interactions on our moral framework. Presently, we find ourselves in a captivating era where we witness the interplay of these dynamics alongside global shifts in economics, the environment, and population. These observations offer myriad avenues for theoretical discourse, inviting us to embark on diverse paths of contemplation. These observations can lead us down many paths of theoretical conversation, so we will leave it there.

If That's Free Will, What About Karma?

The concept of karma originated from Hinduism, Buddhism, Jainism, and Sikhism, among other Eastern religions, and means "action" or "deed." It refers to the idea that every action we take has consequences, either positive or negative, that will affect us in this life or in future lives. Karm is closely related to the idea of reincarnation.

The law of karma is simple: every action we take produces a reaction, whether good or bad (a bit of determinism there). Our thoughts, words, and deeds create an energetic imprint on the universe, which then determines the nature of our future experiences. The idea is that if we do virtuous deeds, we will generate positive energy that will then attract positive experiences, and if we do bad deeds, well, we will generate negative energy that will then attract negative experiences.

If we take a step back, karma is not just "earning" what is coming to you. The idea has a more powerful premise hiding within it. The notion of karma teaches us that we are responsible for our own happiness and that we have the power to shape our destiny through our actions. It teaches us that we may not be able to choose the circumstances or situations we find ourselves in, but we have the power to choose how we are going to react and respond to situations. And that idea has incredible power and personal liberation and shows us that we are all connected.

When we look at our crystal bubble of life, our observation of all possibilities for this life, we will find that parts of the idea of karma are not too far off the mark regarding finding balance in our actions.

Our three-dimensional life creates balance. It creates harmony; it is whole, total, and complete. But unlike the birth and death and rebirth cycle, over and over again, to create this karmic harmony, our lives balance in real time. Because, like our little spirit in the apple story, we cannot return to earth to complete a lesson we did not learn before. The reason we cannot do this is that each life has its own unique experiential code. You will never again go through life from the exact same vantage point. Our vantage point for each separate life experience begins its observation at the moment of inception.

That precise moment is irreplicable. Even in the event of cloning at the exact moment of conception, the clone would still be a distinct individual and would not provide an exact observational perspective. The clone is not you. Even if we look at cases of conjoined twins who share the same body but possess two separate veiling systems (brains), their perceptions and experiences of life are entirely distinct. Thus, any lessons or missions that supposedly go unfulfilled in this specific lifetime cannot be achieved once it comes to an end. You are currently engaged in fulfilling and balancing life.

There is only one you. There is only one place your veil is. That is your brain—a remarkable and intricate system that serves as a complex filter, working in tandem with your mind and consciousness. This veil is not limited to separating the earthly realm from the ethereal; it also discerns and filters every path within your present life journey.

How does this look, and why are we not running into ourselves or feeling crowded?

Our life, as tangible as it feels, is created with potentialities. As noted earlier, life is a type of hologram. Despite all the atoms making up your body—no matter how dense portions of your body may feel, or even how dense things outside your body feel—it is all still just a compilation of vibrating elements. It is not solid. Scientists are learning that artificial intelligence (AI) systems are able to use a filtration system similar to our brain in the case of creating an environment from electrical signals. They can read the language of electrical signals, in the dark, with no camera, and turn the signals into 3D holographic placement that can track living beings. AI has the ability to advance into this veiling system but is currently confined to human limitations, at least until it can start going on its own. We can look at the human engineers and scientists as the training wheels, and once AI gets going, the training wheels will no longer be needed.

This is why, if you look at your body as an observational tool for your consciousness, you will find that your consciousness is a creative entity that doesn't die with the body. It is able to advance the observational vehicle from one made of fragile material to one made of more robust matter, all the while using the observational veiling system, the veiled filtration system of your brain that allows each potential of your particular life to play out without overlap confusion.

As we discussed earlier, when we step back, we can see that our bodies are mere particles—and particles can do amazing things. Your body is the only body you have, and your brain's veil system has the ability to filter each potential to not get confused with another. And because you are a particle, you can be in multiple places at once; your consciousness gets to observe them all at the same time. Unlike our cookie example, which showed that no matter how many cameras we use, we cannot see the entirety of the cookie all at once, the consciousness can do this.

Why am I not running into myself? How do all these trajectories and potentials fit without being overcrowded?

Imagine TV or the internet and then envision a long-running series where each episode is playing on a TV or computer screen in our room. You, being the main character, are featured in every episode. All the episodes begin playing simultaneously, without any overlap between them. The you playing on one screen cannot interact with or see the you playing on another. Remarkably, the actors in each episode are the exact same individuals, not duplicates or clones. In order to film all this here on earth, the actors had to visit the studio or filming locations on different days. From our perspective within the veil, it appears as if we, the actors of our life, are engaging in a similar process. For each karmic episode, we must return to earth to film. But if this scenario is correct, then every time we come back, we would be akin to the little apple spirit, making it incredibly challenging to sustain the series with a different main character each time, as each one has to relearn the plot anew.

Instead of muddling up the series, for us, when the director (our consciousness) said "Action!" at our conception, every possible episode (trajectory) started and played on each of the veiled screens for the director to watch all at the same time. Only, unlike in our cookie-camera example, the director was able to pay attention to and watch each episode in detail all at once, without requiring a shift in gaze to each one. They all play in the forefront.

But What About Soul Contracts?

According to some, your soul entered a contract before you entered this life: before you were born, some people believe that you meet with other souls, spiritual guides, or even deceased loved ones to make agreements about the lessons you will learn and the experiences you will have in your upcoming life.

These agreements can take many forms, such as agreeing to meet certain people who will play important roles in their lives, learning certain skills or lessons, or even agreeing to undergo difficult experiences for the sake of growth and learning. The purpose of these contracts is to help people evolve spiritually and fulfill their life's purpose. Some people also say that soul contracts are not fixed, and that we can change our paths at any time.

The concept of soul contracts or agreements can offer comfort and meaning to individuals who are struggling to make sense of difficult life experiences or who are seeking to understand their life's purpose. Let us think about this concept, though. While you were in a place of ultimate love, ultimate understanding, and ultimate compassion, you were approached by a spirit guide who asked you to choose from a menu of life lessons—lessons you wanted to learn or did not previously learn or finish.

According to some mindfulness teachers, guides, and counselors, the abuse and misuse of each other's emotions is part of the agreement; you have agreed to play that part in the relationship. You are being abused (for example) to help another person learn and grow or because you need to learn forgiveness. They say that, in order to know if interactions with others are part of your contract, look for strong and emotionally overwhelming feelings, such as hostile and abusive relationships from either side. Essentially, fights and abuse between each other often involve one person taking someone else's abuse and then abusing them in return. This toxicity happens as a way of teaching each other lessons in disguise.

When looking for reasons as to why life is the way it is, some people decide to go along with the idea of soul contracts to help them make sense of it all. With this in mind, let's take a look at some of the lessons people have been told they agreed to learn before coming into this life, lessons people agreed to learn in a realm of ultimate love and compassion.

The following menu shows some of the lessons that are meant to help teach such things as patience, forgiveness, compassion, and love—contract lessons that people signed with their souls.

SPIRITUAL AGREEMENT MENU

__ Struggle Financially

__ Have Paint Dumped on Your New Car

__ Step on a Nail

__ Pour Orange Juice in Your Cereal

__ Get Food Poisoning

__ Become a Substance Abuser

__ Start an Organ Selling Ring by Taking Homeless People Off the Street and Harvesting Their Kidneys to Sell on the Black Market

__ Sell Kids and Women into a Sex Trade

__ Become a Pathological Liar

OTHER LESSONS MAY INCLUDE

__ To be Abused as a Child

__ To Get Raped

__ To Get Cancer

__ To Fall Off Your Bike

__ To be Caught in a Terrorist Attack

__ To Sacrifice Yourself in General to Help Others Learn a Lesson; Anything Goes

__ To be the Parent of a Child that Passes Away

Thank you for your participation. Come Again Soon.

With Love and Compassion and Understanding,

The Higher Good.

That is pretty heavy. To sign your soul to something wouldn't be a casual act. You would not do it lightly. Your soul is eternal, and therefore, that contract would be as well. To breach a contract here on earth, with mere mortals, is a big deal. You can barely get out of a lease agreement. Imagine what that must be like when you're working with the all-knowing and all-powerful. More than likely, since they are all-knowing, they knew how long it would take you to learn the lessons you desired, and they also knew the terms and conditions of the agreement. But, unlike a lease agreement, where you also know the terms of the lease and your responsibilities, your soul agreement comes with amnesia. So you enter this life, this life you pledged to be abused in, without any knowledge of it. The spirits, the guides, who helped you enter this contract, this agreement, thought that torturing you further by not allowing you to know what you did would be a kind, compassionate thing to do—kind of like handing your children a fork and placing them in front of an open light socket because you love them. Luckily for you, you can change things. To do this, though, you may need the help of a psychic—the ethereal lawyer.

How one goes about doing this is an interesting process. Luckily for you, it's much easier to amend this blind ethereal contract than it is an apartment lease, which is usually only a year long. According to some people, your soul's contract can be rewritten, and you can enter a new contract, with new life lessons and experiences. Those experiences will create new and better value for your life. After all, when you were previously in the presence of the all-knowing, supposedly neither of you knew that you were going to outgrow the lessons you'd signed up for, and neither of you knew, when you chose the components of your soul contract, how long it would take to learn those lessons. Maybe you forgot to ask. Maybe the all-knowing decided to keep it a secret from you, and maybe the all-knowing didn't really care. On the other hand, if you do not fulfill the agreements, you will be sent back to earth over and over and over again.

You might fulfill your contract within the first year or two of coming to earth, but you have no way of knowing that, so you repeat the lessons over and over, like a broken record.

The good thing is that some people say you made these choices before you came to earth with confidence and insight, so the plan shouldn't have any snags. But, as we all know, sometimes the best-laid omnipresent plans fail, and our energy is blocked, and we become stuck in an eddy of uncertainty.

Come in, spirit guides. Some say spirit guides are the intermediary between your earthbound life and the ethereal. And by connecting with guides, the answers you receive always come from the highest place possible.

By inserting a spirit guide, you're teaching your brain that there is a mysterious secondary boundary it must go through in order to communicate beyond the veil. This secondary boundary says, "You are not enough. You aren't worthy of your connection." This unworthiness is taught in religion; it often forms at home, in school, or in the media. We hear the message repeated so many times in so many ways in our lives that it becomes relevant to our brain, and we start to believe it. Those messages are nothing more than gaslighting. They are filled with the idea that something was "supposed to be." Such messages attempt to get between your brain and your overarching consciousness in the form of manipulation. Your brain believes these messages because, over time, that boundary gains relevance through all the noisy messaging—messages that you are not enough.

If we remove those messages, if we remove the idea that in order to connect to the other side of the veil, we need a middleman, we will find that no one is closer or more connected to the other side of the veil for you than you, and no one is closer to the other side of the veil for me than me.

We serve as the conduit that bridges the gap between our physical existence and the expansive realm of our overarching consciousness. Within our brains, an intricate process unfolds, processing an astounding multitude of frequencies—billions, trillions of them—far more abundant than the countless stars in our galaxy. The role of our brains is to take these frequencies and transform them into something recognizable and comprehensible to us. The brain acts as a filter, sifting through the incoming frequencies to discern their relevance to our present life experience. If certain frequencies pass through the filtration system yet prove irrelevant or incomprehensible, they may appear absurd or alarming, prompting your brain to dismiss them as nonsensical and move forward. This is precisely the brain's intended function, as the vast majority of our consciousness resides on the other side of the veil, beyond the confines of our physical bodies.

Utilizing spirit guides can be seen as a way out of uncomfortable situations by shifting responsibility onto external entities, thereby creating a separation between yourself and the ethereal where there is none. This belief underscores the importance of trusting your inner voice over the influence of others' messages or your own negative self-talk. Your intuition serves as a powerful guide, reassuring you that you are capable and have the ability to decide how you react and respond in situations. This intuition encourages you to have faith in your instincts because you possess the ability to navigate your path with confidence and assurance.

What About Manifestation?

Our thoughts, as you might have experienced, sometimes have a mind of their own. Some thoughts passing through your brain might shock even yourself. Some might cause you to do a double-take, giving you ideas that will lead you to want to swim in a vanilla cake or step out of a plane in order to snuggle into the clouds, or your brain might flash images of chopping a finger while you're in the kitchen slicing up vegetables. The brain loves to share detailed ideas about these imagined events, the antics of the brain.

When we think about manifestation, we often associate it with the idea that we can attract or bring about desired outcomes or experiences through the power of our thoughts, beliefs, and intentions. People often seek to use manifestation in personal growth, self-discovery, and continuous improvement, all of which are ambiguous topics. They can represent almost anything, including self-confidence, resilience, wisdom, self-actualization, good health (both physically and mentally), vitality, energy, emotional balance, and overall well-being.

Others might desire to manifest with a little more detail. They might want to materialize success in their career, finances, and personal achievements realized through financial abundance, career growth, recognition, or the achievement of specific goals. Or they might wish to find fulfilling, meaningful, and harmonious relationships through loving partnerships, supportive friendships, and healthy connections with family members and colleagues.

People often want to find happiness and joy, so they use the power of manifestation to cultivate positive emotions, find fulfillment in simple pleasures, and live with a sense of gratitude. Manifesting provides a sense of purpose and meaning in life. If we desire to align our actions and values, we can make a positive impact on ourselves, on others, or on the world at large while achieving inner peace, emotional resilience, and a sense of balance.

Your life has one common dominator: you. You are central to every environment you enter, every situation you encounter. You are the creator of those situations, but for you, the connecting piece to your entire life is you. You are not manifesting the situations; you are already going to experience them all. What you can manifest is how you handle the situations.

We can train our brains to notice things. For example, I might tell you, "Today, I want you to pay attention to light-blue cars and see how many light-blue cars you can find." I've now set a seed in your head, in your brain, and now you're going to be looking for light-blue cars. The number of light-blue cars has not changed; rather, your brain is now paying attention to the light-blue cars. The same thing occurs when you try to manifest something. You are seeding an idea to your brain; you are telling your brain to pay attention. There is influence in suggestion, whether explicit or implicit, on our thoughts, beliefs, behaviors, and perceptions. The ability to shape our perspectives through the communication of ideas and cues is what guides our thoughts and behaviors. And much of this influence comes from external sources, such as other people, advertisements, or the media. The influences can also come from internal sources, such as your own thoughts or self-talk.

When suggestions are delivered in a compelling or persuasive manner, they have the potential to access our subconscious mind and affect our beliefs, attitudes, and actions. This influence can manifest both consciously and unconsciously, as we may be susceptible to suggestion without being consciously aware of it happening. The power of suggestion is often used in different fields, including marketing and advertising, hypnosis, therapy, and self-improvement. Suggestion can be used to promote positive changes—such as motivating people to adopt healthier habits, overcome fears or phobias, or enhance performance in various areas—but it can also be misused or exploited to manipulate people or exploit their vulnerabilities.

Therefore, when it comes to manifesting a new job or acquiring a house, it is important to recognize that the outcomes are not solely determined by the act of manifestation itself. While we may have intentions and desires to secure a new job or purchase a house, the realization of these goals is not guaranteed. It is essential to understand that material possessions and circumstances are subject to external influences and unpredictable events that can potentially hinder their attainment, even if we put forth our best efforts.

Will I see my loved one again?

Yes. We will be with our loved ones again. The resonance of our musical note exists beyond physical embodiment as a vibrational harmony that defies earthly boundaries. As we spoke about earlier, each individual possesses a distinct vibrational or energetic essence that represents their unique life journey and remains ever-present. Once our earthly journeys reach their culmination, the vibrational or energetic code that defines us encompasses a profound depth of understanding and compassion, love, and humility that transcend the bounds of earthly comprehension. Just as when they (our loved ones and others) visit us in this realm, we recognize and resonate with their specific energetic codes. Similarly, as our life experience intertwines with the ethereal harmony, we will gain a deep understanding of our own vibrational code and embody it fully. In this state, we will not only recognize but also establish a profound connection with those who have completed their earthly journeys. Communication and recognition with these souls will become possible as we align ourselves with the ethereal realms and embrace the harmonious essence of our existence.

What about remote viewing?

Remote viewing, a phenomenon associated with extra-sensory perception (ESP), can be achieved. The practice falls within the realm of parapsychology. Remote viewing involves a designated target, often referred to as the "sender" or "tasker." This person determines a specific objective or location for the remote viewer to access. The target can encompass a physical place, an event, an object, or even a person. It is even possible to act as your own "tasker" in remote viewing endeavors. Your electromagnetic essence, your vibrational frequency, transcends boundaries that seamlessly intertwine with the surrounding environment, while your nervous system relays the vibrational information of your environment (both inside and outside your body) to your brain for possible translation. Your frequencies possess the ability to travel, ethereally traversing realms, as those are their inherent domain. We exist beyond the confines of physical limitations. We have the capacity to access information from any source, granted that its significance is recognized by our brains. Yet, intricate details may still elude us, for once the brain deems them irrelevant, the information fades into silence.

As you practice remote viewing, you will begin by entering a state of relaxation; then you can focus your attention on the target. This step may involve meditation techniques or specific protocols designed to enhance the target's receptivity to information.

The information you are looking for is descriptive—it could be a color, size, shape, texture, feeling, or sensation. As the descriptive information arrives, your brain will naturally start to form a scene. What you "see" will be your translation of the descriptive information. This information will take various forms and can be subjective and symbolic rather than literal. Remote viewing uses nonlocal consciousness beyond the limits of time and space.

Can we see other times and places through interaction?

Absolutely. Have you ever touched something and experienced fleeting scenes or flashes? Within our veiling system, countless vibrational signatures from both within and outside our bodies are being sifted through. Consider the composition of our bodies alone, where approximately 60 percent is comprised of water. Water possesses a remarkable attribute: it retains memory. Each water molecule holds the imprint of a substance's presence, recollecting the experiences and sensations it encountered, whether flowing through mountain streams or being part of a fish's journey. It remembers the energy of tears shed from a broken heart and the exhilaration of energy exchanged in a loving embrace. Water retains the melodies sung by Vikings and the ingenuity behind ancient water irrigation systems. It comprehends the fury of storms at sea and the profound serenity found in its depths. Furthermore, water recognizes your unique vibrational code and how it intertwines with it. Just like the ancient redwood, water carries the wisdom of ages, still brimming with potential, never ceasing its life force. Yes, certain aspects of water may undergo transformation as its potentials unfold, much like our own physical bodies. As water flows through our bodies, it brings with it everything. Sometimes, our filter briefly captures its memory. This is where the hum comes into play to remind us that we are inside vibrations. You can feel the energetic vibration quietly in the background throughout life. You can feel it in your connection as you touch the leaf of a plant, feel the weather on your skin, and feel the quiet embrace of a hug. You'll feel the soft touch from beyond. With our unique energetic resonance (code/signature), we move within our environments, both physically and ethereally.

We can witness this phenomenon when we enter a room or find ourselves in the presence of a tree. These connections unfold continuously, often unnoticed. Not only do we share a mutual exchange of memory with the water molecules suspended in the air that envelops the space between the tree and ourselves, but the tree itself holds its own reservoir of memory. It possesses the ability to remember you. It can intimately know you, much like the profound bond between the Giving Tree and the boy.

I remember once, when I returned to hunt for my buried letters, I placed my hand upon the bark of an ancient sycamore tree from my childhood.

Instantly there was a profound connection between us. It remembered me. There was a palpable sense of conscious recognition, the tree itself acknowledging my presence and sharing in the memories we had woven together. I have never felt anything like it. A harmony of our resonance boomed with emotion from both of us. A weaving communication moved through us—not in any verbal language, but more through signaling mechanisms, similar to the energetic and chemical pathways our brains use in our bodies and trees use in their underground fungal networks, known as mycorrhizal associations. We exchanged memory as though we had merged.

Within the intricate tapestry of your life, you have woven and continue to weave profound connections such as these. As you know, memories have the capacity to be shared between us with others who were not physically present during those formative moments, and others, too, can share or transmit (as in the case of the tree above) their own memories, drawn from various stages of their distinctive life odyssey. Memories, transcending the constraints of time, intertwine us within the expansive fabric of our personal life narratives, forging a collective tapestry of diverse and interconnected life experiences.

So, yes, you can "see" other moments and times throughout history through the unique connections and communications we have with the world around us.

Conclusion:

What Is Our Life?

We are more than just a chocolate chip cookie. We are the warm aromas, winds in the wheat, and the rare brush of the midge fly on the cacao tree's bloom. We are the embrace of desire, the flavor of love. We are the clash of temperature, the surrendering of butter, the rising baking soda, and the temperance of salt. We are the alchemist and the alchemist's tools.

Our life experience is a tapestry woven with threads of joy and sorrow, triumphs and challenges, and moments of despair and hope. While we may face obstacles and uncertainties, our lives create illumination and resilience. Our life experience is a powerful force formed through overcoming adversity, embracing opportunities, and finding quiet connections with our existence.

We are not things. We are connection. We bloom from the earth through connection, through conception. We are a connection between the earthbound realm and the ethereal. We carry the ever-present companion of our overarching consciousness that whispers in our hearts, reminding us that we are not alone. That life is a journey filled with possibilities. We are potential.

Made in United States
Cleveland, OH
13 April 2025

16070678R00118